CRIME SOLVERS

Mystery in the Morgue

BE A PATHOLOGIST

by Alix Wood

 Gareth Stevens
PUBLISHING

Please visit our website, **www.garethstevens.com**. For a free color
catalog of all our high-quality books, call toll free 1-800-542-2595
or fax 1-877-542-2596

Cataloging-in-Publication Data

Names: Wood, Alix.
Title: Mystery in the morgue: be a pathologist / Alix Wood.
Description: New York : Gareth Stevens Publishing, 2018. | Series: Crime solvers |
    Includes index.
Identifiers: ISBN 9781538206393 (pbk.) | ISBN 9781538206331 (library bound) |
    ISBN 9781538206218 (6 pack)
Subjects: LCSH: Forensic pathology--Juvenile literature. | Criminal investigation--
    Juvenile literature. | Forensic sciences--Juvenile literature.
Classification: LCC RA1063.4 W66 2018 | DDC 614.1--dc23

First Edition

Published in 2018 by
Gareth Stevens Publishing
111 East 14th Street, Suite 349
New York, NY 10003

Copyright © 2018 Alix Wood Books

Produced for Gareth Stevens by Alix Wood Books
Designed by Alix Wood
Editor: Eloise Macgregor
Consultant: Stacey Deville, MFS, Texas Forensic Investigative Consultants

Photo credits: Cover, 1, 4, 6, 7, 8, 10, 11, 12, 15, 17, 18, 20, 21, 22, 24, 25, 26, 27 top, 28, 29, 30, 31,
32, 33, 34, 35, 36, 38, 40, 41, 42, 43 © Adobe Stock Images, 9 © Harry James, 13 © Deborah Harding,
16, 27 bottom, 39 © Alix Wood

Printed in the United States of America
CPSIA compliance information: Batch #CS17GS For further information contact Gareth Stevens, New York, New York at 1-800-542-2595.

CONTENTS

Call the Pathologist... 4

Meet a Forensic Pathologist 6

What Do Forensic Pathologists Do?.............8

SCIENCE DETECTIVE Who Is the Victim? 10

A Little Bit of Doubt 12

SCIENCE DETECTIVE Pathologist's Eye View 14

An Identity...16

The Time of Death 18

SCIENCE DETECTIVE Is Everyone the Same? 20

The Body's Secrets..................................22

SCIENCE DETECTIVE Know Your Insides Inside Out?. 24

Secrets in the Soil..................................26

SCIENCE DETECTIVE What Plant Left That?.............28

A Fall, Or a Push? 30

SCIENCE DETECTIVE How Do You Get DNA? 32

The Crime Scene....................................34

Meeting the Family..................................36

SCIENCE DETECTIVE Rotten Experiment! 38

Getting Ready For Court..........................40

The Verdict..42

Glossary and Answers..............................44

Want to Be a Forensic Pathologist?...........46

Further Information 47

Index..48

call the pathologist...

The sun is rising on a summer morning in July, and Joe Malloney is walking along East Street to his early shift at work. He crosses the street and sees a woman lying on the sidewalk. Did she collapse? Did a car hit her and knock her down? He goes to take a look...

DISPATCHER: Emergency 911. What is the location of your emergency?

JOE: I'm on East Street, near the crossroads with 17th. There's a woman that looks as if she's been hit by a car.

DISPATCHER: What is your name, caller?

JOE: I'm Joe Malloney. I'm just on my way to work at the printers on 19th.

DISPATCHER: Is the woman breathing?

JOE: No. She looks pretty dead...

Reporting Officer's Notes

6:22 am: Dispatch received a 911 call about a **hit-and-run**, near the corner of East Street and 17th. The caller identified himself as Joe Malloney.

Unit 324 was **dispatched** and arrived at the scene at 6:31 am. The officers found what appeared to be a road accident **victim** lying on the sidewalk. They roped off the scene and asked for medical assistance. The woman appeared to be dead

7:44 am: Detectives arrived at the scene. A medical team checked over the body to be sure there was nothing that they could do. The **coroner** arrived a few minutes later and certified the death. It looked like a straightforward road accident. The pathologist, Prisha Gupta, is called. She is on her way.

Case File

The detectives search the street for any sign of a car that could have hit the victim. They ask around the neighborhood to find out if anyone heard tires squeal or saw anything unusual. This early in the morning, there aren't many people around. Once the pathologist looks at the body, they'll have a better idea what happened.

Solve It!

What signs would the detectives look for to convince them it was a car accident?

a) black skid marks on the road surface

b) pieces of broken glass or plastic

c) a and b

Answers on page 45

meet a forensic pathologist

Prisha Gupta is already awake. The beautiful sunrise lighting up her bedroom has woken her up early. She has a full workday planned, so she gets ready quickly.

Prisha grabs her bag and car keys and heads out into the sunshine. Her phone buzzes just as she gets into her car. She has just enough time to get to the **crime scene** and still make it to her first meeting.

Name: Prisha Gupta

Job: Forensic pathologist

Education: After high school it takes around 15 years to become a forensic pathologist. Prisha spent 4 years studying for a degree, then 4 years at medical school followed by 5 years at a hospital. Then she spent 2 years taking pathology exams and getting a fellowship!

Career:
Prisha has only been working as a forensic pathologist for about one year. It is her first job in the field.

Favorite school subject: Biology

Favorite part of her job: Getting to work with all kinds of people, such as lawyers, police officers, forensic experts, and members of the public.

Worst part of her job: Waiting around for hours in court for her turn to give **evidence**, when she could be doing something more useful.

Most interesting case: Prisha worked on an interesting case while she was training. A man had died of knife wounds. Investigators believed his wife murdered him with a kitchen knife she always used. When Prisha examined the knife wound, it was obvious that a hunting knife must have been used, so his wife was found innocent.

what do forensic pathologists do?

Pathology is the study of diseases and what causes them. The word "forensic" means to do with solving crime. Forensic pathologists try to discover a cause of death in cases where the death was sudden or when the police suspect the death may be **suspicious**.

Solve It!

Police are called to a scene. A dead man at the foot of a ladder has a head wound. Who has the final say on how the man died?

a) the detective

b) a forensic pathologist

c) a doctor

Answers on page 45

Prisha usually goes to a crime scene to see if anything there might help her discover the cause of death. Detectives have already examined the scene before Prisha gets there. They'll have recorded and collected any evidence. Detectives tell the forensic pathologist what they have found. They will show Prisha any evidence, and talk through everything they have noticed. Some evidence can be very helpful in determining the cause of death.

EVIDENCE BAG CHALLENGE

Sometimes a cause of death is really obvious. Imagine that you are Prisha and you arrive at the crime scenes below. What do you think are the obvious causes of death in each case?

Crime Scene 1: Prisha arrives on a sunny afternoon to find a man's body at the bottom of a cliff. Above him is a length of broken rope. A detective shows her an evidence bag. It contains another piece of broken rope that was found in the man's hands. Cause of death?

a) he died from a fall   b) he died from cold

Crime Scene 2: Detectives call Prisha to an alleyway. A woman is lying in a pool of blood with a knife sticking out of her chest. There are no other marks on the body. Cause of death?

a) she died from poisoning   b) she died from a knife wound

Answers on page 45

Who Is the Victim?

One of the most important jobs at a murder scene is to quickly work out the identity of the victim. Who they are will usually give clues to who might have killed them. People can be identified in a number of ways.

Sometimes, simply finding some form of ID on the person can tell detectives who the victim is. If detectives can't find any ID, forensic pathologists can sometimes help. Details that they find on the person's body can help identify them.

Solve It!

Imagine you had lost your memory and didn't know who you were. Which information below might give a pathologist a really good clue to help you find your identity?

a) a scar from an operation

b) your eye color

c) your clothes

Answers on page 45

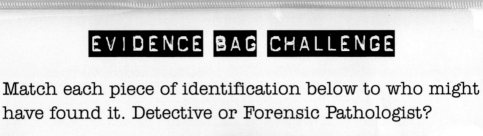

EVIDENCE BAG CHALLENGE

Match each piece of identification below to who might have found it. Detective or Forensic Pathologist?

Detective or **Forensic Pathologist**

Answers on page 45

A LITTLE BIT OF DOUBT

Prisha arrives at East Street and goes to talk to the detectives. She examines the body. From her injuries, it certainly looks like a car may have hit the woman. The detectives believe the death was probably caused by a hit-and-run. A hit-and-run is a road accident where the driver does not stop to report the accident or help the victim. It is a serious crime.

The detectives talk it through with Prisha. They would be more convinced it was a hit-and-run if they could see signs of an accident, apart from just the victim herself.

At the Crime Scene

Prisha usually tries to establish the cause of death, the time of death, and the manner of death at the scene. She will always do an **autopsy** later, to double-check any of her findings. An autopsy is the thorough examination of the body done by the forensic pathologist.

POLICE LINE - DO NOT CROSS

Before the body can be moved, the investigating team has to be sure it has recorded all the information possible from the crime scene. Evidence can sometimes be lost when a body is moved. This is where the Crime Scene Investigation (**CSI**) team moves in...

Finding Evidence

The streets are getting busy now with more and more people on their way to work. The detectives and Prisha need to work quickly. They can't keep the road shut forever. As they can't be 100 percent sure of the cause of death, detectives treat it as a murder scene.

The Crime Scene Investigators get to work. They collect anything that might be important — fibers, hair, glass, even tiny flakes of paint! Everything is bagged up, labeled, and sent off to be examined. They also record exactly where they found each item. The crime scene team draws a diagram of the scene and labels it. They photograph the scene, too.

SCIENCE DETECTIVE

Pathologist's Eye View

While the CSI team is collecting evidence, Prisha examines the crime scene. Different people will often spot different things. It is good to have a variety of experts at work.

A pathologist will usually concentrate on any injuries to the body, and what, or who, might have caused them. Forensic pathologists can usually tell how long the person has been dead, and whether they died at the scene or somewhere else. Can you predict which two of the four facts below Prisha may have noticed at the scene?

1 The victim had soil in a wound on her head.

2 The diner opposite opened at 5 am. Maybe someone there saw something?

3 There is a CCTV camera pointing at the street corner.

4 The victim was dead for around two hours.

Solve It!

The victim had soil in her hair. She was found on the pavement with no soil anywhere around. What might the team think or do about that?

a) Look around the local area for anywhere soil may be found.

b) Don't worry about it. She may have already had the soil in her hair.

c) A truck carrying dirt may have jolted by and some fell on her.

Answers on page 45

EVIDENCE BAG CHALLENGE

You will need: some friends to interview, paper, pens

Everyone sees things differently. Test your friends' powers of observation. How accurate are they as witnesses? How much do people remember days after an event takes place?

1 Look at the picture below. Write down some questions that you could ask that would test your friends' memories. Ask questions that need definite answers, questions like "Which boys were throwing paper?" Don't ask questions that need an **opinion**, such as "Who do you think is the worst bully?"

2 Have your friends look at the picture below for a few minutes. Give each of them your questions and note down their answers. How accurate were they?

3 After a week, ask them the same questions again without showing them the photo. How much have they forgotten?

An Identity

No form of I.D. was found with the body. The police are baffled. Detectives have been checking any reports of missing people. No one has been reported missing that matches the description of the dead woman. They are beginning to wonder if they will ever discover who she is.

Then Prisha glances up. Above the street there is an apartment building. On some of the apartment's balconies were beautiful, colorful window boxes full of flowers.

Top Tip

Always look up and down and all around when searching a crime scene. Not everything is going to be found at eye level.

Solve It!

Why do you think that Prisha was so interested in the window boxes?

a) she has always loved flowers

b) she wanted to look at something beautiful, as a break

c) the window boxes would have soil in them

Answers on page 45

Prisha sees that one of the window boxes on the second floor looks broken. The detectives head into the apartment block. They start knocking on people's doors, to see if anyone had heard or seen anything suspicious. A lot of apartments are empty — the people have already left for work. No one they speak to on the second floor heard anything unusual.

Detectives worked their way up the building. On the fourth floor they spoke to a couple who heard a banging sound from apartment 44 early this morning. They hadn't thought it was important. They thought, just like everyone else, that the poor woman on the street had been hit by a car.

The Time of Death

One of the most important jobs of the forensic pathologist is to try to estimate the time of death. This can really help the detectives on the case. Once detectives know the time of death and can trace where the victim would have been at that time, this information can often lead to the killer.

A common way to estimate the time of death is to check the victim's body temperature. A body loses 1.5 degrees per hour until they reach the temperature of the environment around them. Body temperature is usually around 98 degrees Fahrenheit (37 degrees Celsius). Pathologists have to bear in mind that a dead body's temperature will drop more slowly if the body was left in a cold place. In a hot place, the body temperature may even rise, not drop.

Top Tip

It may not be very scientific, but a forensic pathologist will often look for one very simple clue. If the victim was wearing a watch and it is broken, what time does it say?

EVIDENCE BAG CHALLENGE

The human body is around 60 percent water. Different surrounding temperatures affect how quickly or slowly a body cools after death. How quickly does water cool down when kept at different temperatures?

You will need: three freezer-safe bowls, water, pen and paper, a **thermometer** if you have one

1. Half fill three bowls with lukewarm water. Place one bowl in the fridge, one bowl in the freezer, and leave one bowl out at room temperature.

2. After ten minutes, take a temperature reading. You can just put your finger in the bowls if you don't have a thermometer! Has the temperature of the water changed? Write down your results.

	ten minutes	one hour
fridge	still warm	cold
freezer	cold	icy
room	warm	warm

3. After an hour, take another reading. Can you put your finger or thermometer in each bowl, or has the water changed in any way? Write down your results. Why do you think we keep food in cold places? Would a cold day help keep a body fresher, too?

Solve It!

Can you work out our victim's time of death? Remember — body temperature is about 98 degrees Fahrenheit and a body loses 1.5 degrees each hour after death. The weather was mild. The victim's temperature at 7:20 am was 95 degrees Fahrenheit.

a) the time of death was 5:20 am

b) the time of death was 6:20 am

Answers on page 45

Is Everyone the Same?

People are different. You probably know some people that seem to always either feel too hot or too cold. Some people actually do cool down faster than others. Thin people, young children, and the elderly may all feel the cold quicker than others. Naturally, if someone is wearing thick clothing, they will cool down slower, too.

The same is true with dead bodies. A plump woman wrapped up in warm clothes will take longer to cool down than a thin old lady. Forensic pathologists must bear this in mind when they estimate a time of death. To be safe, times of death are usually written as "between this time and that time."

Solve It!

Which of the factors below might slow a body cooling down?

a) the victim was a 40-year-old man

b) the victim wore a t-shirt and jeans

c) the victim was wrapped in a sleeping bag

Answers on page 45

Could you be a forensic pathologist? Work out the time of death from the crime scenes described below. Remember, body temperature is usually around 98 degrees Fahrenheit and loses 1.5 degrees an hour.

It's a December afternoon in downtown Crimeville. A body is found at 4 pm in an apartment block. The heating in the apartment is set to 70 degrees Fahrenheit all day. The body's temperature is recorded to be 98 degrees Fahrenheit. How long have they been dead?

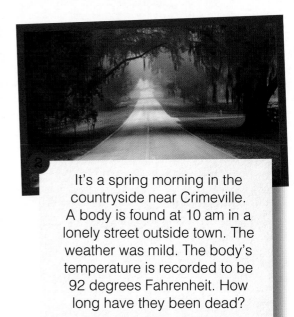

It's a spring morning in the countryside near Crimeville. A body is found at 10 am in a lonely street outside town. The weather was mild. The body's temperature is recorded to be 92 degrees Fahrenheit. How long have they been dead?

a) cannot be sure from temperature alone

b) less than one hour

c) around four hours

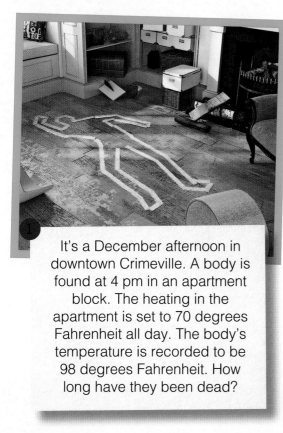

It's a fall day in Crimeville. A body is found at 12 noon in a house by the school. The heating had been turned up high to 104 degrees Fahrenheit. The body's temperature is recorded to be 104 degrees Fahrenheit. How long had they been dead?

The Body's Secrets

Once the team has finished gathering all the evidence, Prisha takes the body back to do an autopsy. It may seem gruesome to imagine a job where you examine dead bodies. Prisha finds doing autopsies really interesting, though. It is like solving a puzzle.

Prisha already had other autopsies to do that day. Forensic pathologists investigate any death that might be suspicious. Bodies that appear to have died from an accident, from the person harming themselves, or from dying unexpectedly must all be investigated. It's possible they were actually murdered.

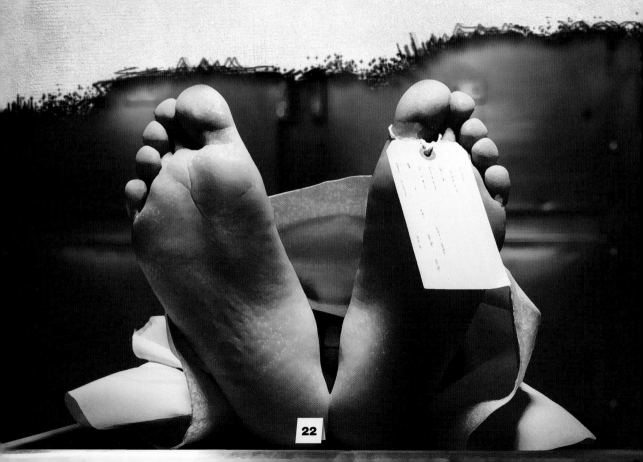

Eventually, Prisha starts examining her East Street victim. She wants to solve this mystery. Did her victim really get hit by a car? Or did she fall, or was she pushed? Prisha loves a puzzle. She finds a two strands of hair in the victim's clenched hand. Could she have grabbed at whoever pushed her off the balcony? She sends the hair to the lab for **analysis**.

Top Tip

Plenty of information can be found by just looking at the body. Forensic pathologists will always look for obvious signs of injury on the outside, before they take a look inside.

EVIDENCE BAG CHALLENGE

Try out your forensic pathology skills. Can you match the autopsy evidence to the cause of death from some of Prisha's earlier cases?

Autopsy 1: Prisha finds some water in the victim's lungs.

Autopsy 2: Prisha finds traces of a deadly chemical in the victim's hair roots.

Autopsy 3: Prisha finds a puncture wound in the victim's heart and a wound in their chest.

Stabbed!

drowned!

Poisoned!

Know Your Insides Inside Out?

Forensic pathologists have to have an excellent knowledge of the human body and how it works. Do you know your liver from your large intestine? Read the description of each body part below. Can you work out which body part is being described?

1. This is one of the most important organs in the human body. It pumps blood around our body through blood vessels.

2. This organ is the control center for your body. It is protected by your skull.

3. These organs transport oxygen from the air you breathe into your bloodstream.

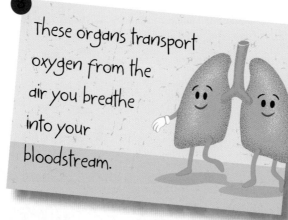

Can you match the body parts to where they are found on the body?

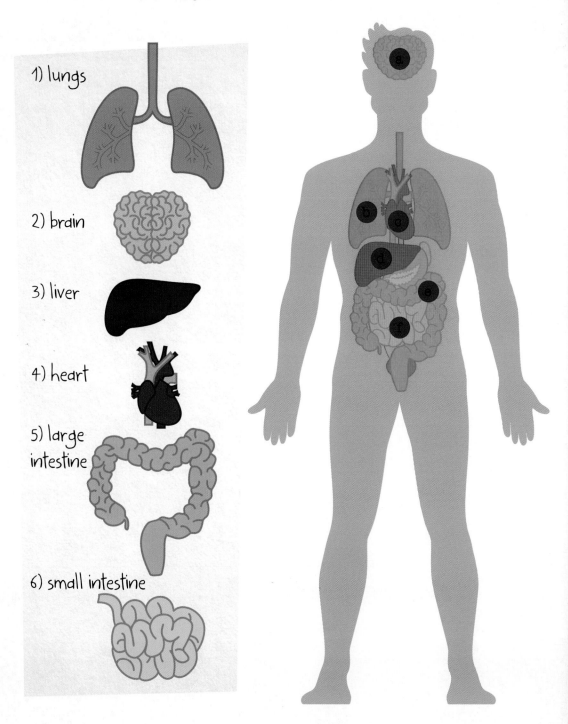

1) lungs

2) brain

3) liver

4) heart

5) large intestine

6) small intestine

The answers are on page 45.

secrets in the soil

Prisha spent several hours examining the victim. She could tell from the victim's injuries that she had suffered a blow to the head. Just as Prisha had noticed at the crime scene, the cut on the victim's head had soil in it. Prisha looked at the soil from the wound and the soil sample detectives had sent to her from the window box on the second floor. They looked very similar.

Top Tip

Soil samples can be so unique that sometimes a sample can be traced to an exact location.

Soil Specialist

Prisha calls in the experts. Peter Trelawne is a forensic soil specialist. Soil can contain dead plant material and microbes only found in certain areas. Peter studies the soil under a microscope to get details about the soil's contents. He then looks at databases with information about soil types in different regions to help pinpoint the area the soil may have come from. In this case, Peter just needs to compare the soil from the victim's hair with the soil sample found at the apartment. It's a match!

EVIDENCE BAG CHALLENGE

Be a forensic soil specialist and see what your local soil is made of.

You will need: a jar with a lid, soil, water, masking tape, a marker

1. Half fill the jar with soil. Wet the soil so it is sticky mud. Place a strip of masking tape on the outside of the jar and mark where the soil comes to.

2. Fill the jar with water. Put on the lid and shake the jar. Let the soil settle for 40 seconds. Mark the level of any settled soil at the bottom. This will be the sand in the soil.

3. Wait six hours and mark the level of soil again. Between your sand mark and this mark is how much **silt** you have in your soil.

4. See if soil from another neighborhood gives you the same results.

What Plant Left That?

Prisha has studied for years to learn everything she can about the human body. Sometimes, though, her job needs her to be able to identify some other unusual objects found on a victim. While Prisha was examining the victim's head wound, she found some tiny, black objects. They looked like plant seeds. She asks a forensic **botanist** who says they are geranium seeds. There were geraniums in the window box.

Forensic Botany

Botany is the study of plants. Forensic botanists use their knowledge of plants to solve crime. A rare plant growing at a crime scene could help catch a killer. Pollen is a powder-like substance released by plants when they reproduce. Rare pollen grains found on a suspect's clothes, hair, or skin could prove that they were at a crime scene.

Different areas produce unique combinations of pollens, even if the pollen is all from common plants. Botanists can sometimes match this unique mix to a location. Plants can give away where a victim might be buried, too. Certain plants like to grow where soil has been freshly dug.

Could you recognize any plant seeds? Match the seed, nut, or pit to the right flower, tree, or fruit, below.

1 dandelion

a

2 oak tree

b

3 sunflower

c

4 pumpkin

d

5 peach

e

A Fall, or a Push?

Prisha was now fairly sure this was no car accident. The soil and seed samples proved the victim hit her head on the window box. The injuries Prisha found during the autopsy could easily have been caused by a fall from the 4th floor. Did the victim fall by accident or was she pushed?

Detectives discovered the victim was a fashion designer named Sarah-Ann Preedy. She lived in apartment 44 with her husband. Did he push her? Or was someone else in the apartment? One way to tell who has been at a crime scene is to search for hair samples, or traces of body fluids, such as sweat, saliva, or blood. The killer may have left some **DNA** behind.

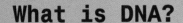

DNA looks a little like a twisted ladder.

What is DNA?

DNA is a substance found in a body's cells. Each person's DNA is unique. Anyone arrested for a crime has a sample of their DNA taken and the results are stored on a database. Police can check the database when DNA is found at a crime scene. They can also take DNA samples from any suspects, to see if there is a match.

The "rungs" of DNA's ladder structure are made with pairs of either adenine, thymine, cytosine, and guanine. They are known by their first letter: A, T, C, and G. A only pairs with T, and C only pairs with G!

Solve It!

Even using just four letters and pairing them in this strict way, DNA can still make an almost infinite number of different patterns because DNA contains millions of these pairs. Because of this, each person's DNA is unique. The DNA below left was found on the hair samples Prisha found in the victim's hand. Can you find a match from the four people known to have visited the apartment that day?

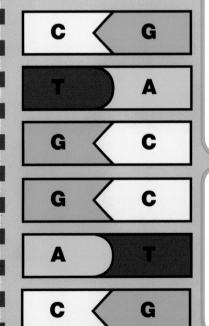

Husband:
John Preedy

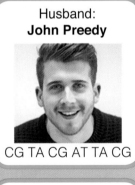

CG TA CG AT TA CG

Building Super:
William Twogood

CG AA CG GC AT CG

Sarah-Ann's brother:
James Proctor

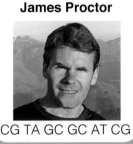

CG TA GC GC AT CG

Pizza delivery guy:
Sam York

CC TA GC GC AT CG

Answers on page 45

How Do You Get DNA?

Police take saliva swabs from peoples' cheeks to collect DNA for their databases. Only 0.1 percent of DNA code varies from person to person. This is the part of the code forensic scientists test. Analysts often copy the DNA using a thermal cycler, like the one pictured below. The cycler raises or lowers the temperature in a special order. This separates and boosts the DNA, and creates copies of the strand. Having plenty of DNA makes it easier to analyze.

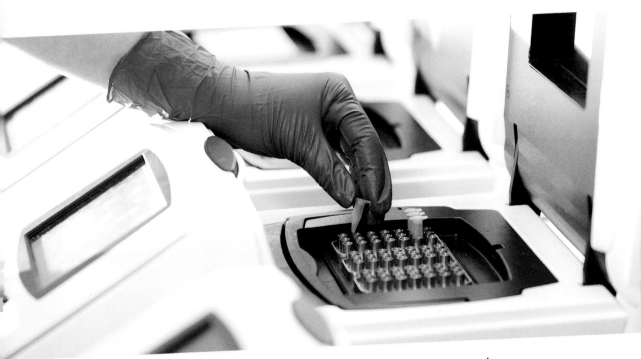

Want to see your own DNA?

Try this amazing experiment on the next page.

EVIDENCE BAG CHALLENGE

You will need: a tablespoon, a teaspoon, salt, a measuring jug, water, liquid soap, a small bowl and cup, a test tube or narrow jar, something to stir with, rubbing alcohol or isopropyl alcohol

1. Dissolve 1 tablespoon of salt in 1 cup (250 ml) of water to make a salt solution. Put ¼ teaspoon of the salt solution into the test tube.

2. Mix 1 tablespoon of liquid soap with 3 tablespoons of water in a small bowl to make a soap solution.

3. Swish 1 teaspoon of tap water around your mouth for around 30 seconds. Spit this into a small cup. Add the spit water and ¼ teaspoon of the soap solution to the test tube.

4. Cover the test tube. If it doesn't have a stopper, you can use plastic film. Gently turn the test tube until it is almost upside down, several times, to mix everything together. Be gentle so you don't make any bubbles.

5. Remove the stopper. Drizzle 1 teaspoon of rubbing alcohol so it runs down the inside of the jar. It should form a layer on top of the mixture.

6. You should now see a white, stringy layer forming. This is your DNA!

7. Use your stirrer to gently pull out the strings of DNA and have a look!

a test tube

The crime scene

Apartment 44 was now being treated as a crime scene. After finishing her other work for the day, Prisha went to the apartment. She wanted to check a few things that had been troubling her since the autopsy. She was also curious why Sarah-Ann went onto the balcony so early in the morning.

The detectives showed her around. There was no sign of a break-in. The apartment door was locked. The door to the balcony was open. The apartment was tidy, with no sign of a struggle. There was a faint smell of smoke in the hall, and the remains of a burnt pizza box.

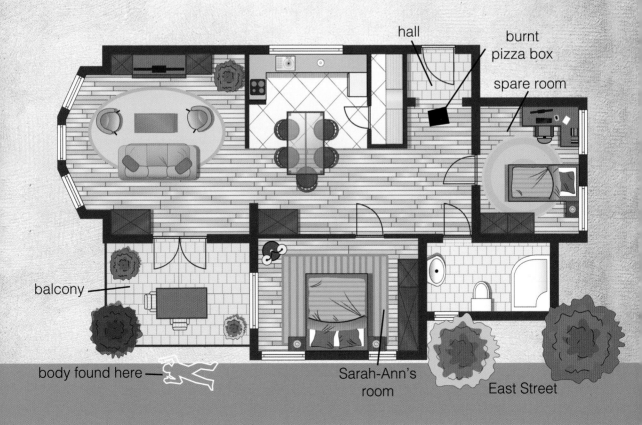

hall

burnt pizza box

spare room

balcony

body found here

Sarah-Ann's room

East Street

Prisha had found something unusual on the victim when she did her autopsy. Sarah-Ann's nostrils had small traces of soot in them. The smell of smoke in the hall made Prisha suspicious. When she had examined Sarah-Ann's lungs at the autopsy, she could see that Sarah-Ann had never smoked.

Top Tip

Teamwork is important. Prisha talks through the case with the detectives. Each profession will notice different things at a crime scene.

Solve It!

Have a look at the plan of the crime scene. Why do you think Sarah-Ann went onto the balcony so early in the morning?

a) a small fire in the hall woke Sarah-Ann, and blocked her main exit, so she ran to the balcony

b) Sarah-Ann had been smoking a cigarette in the hall. Her brother was staying in the spare room. She heard her brother get up, so she went to finish her cigarette on the balcony

Answers on page 45

The detectives check the smoke detector on the hall ceiling. The battery had been removed!

meeting the family

The victim's family often asks to meet the forensic pathologist. They like to find out as much as they can about how their loved one may have died. It is a difficult but important part of the job for Prisha.

Sarah-Ann's husband:
John Preedy

Sarah-Ann's brother:
James Proctor

Sarah-Ann's parents:
George and Helen Proctor

Case File

The Manner of Death

As well as deciding what the cause of death is, pathologists also have to decide on the "manner" of death. Was the death a murder, or **suicide**, or an accident, or from natural causes? If Prisha can't be sure, she calls the death "undetermined". This is usually one of the most important things the victim's family want to know. Why did their loved one die? Is anyone to blame?

What do you think Prisha will write on this case file?

a) murder
b) natural
c) accident
d) undetermined

Answers on page 45

Rotten Experiment!

Have you ever examined a pumpkin a few days after Halloween? The heat from the candles makes it quickly start to rot. Different conditions affect how quickly a body **decomposes**, too. Pathologists learn how to tell how long a person has been dead by looking at the changes that occur to a body under different conditions.

In this experiment, see for yourself how meat decomposes in different conditions. It can get smelly. Make sure you get permission from whoever looks after you before you try this experiment!

You will need: three chicken drumsticks, some foil, a container of water, an outdoor space away from neighbors, a wire container to keep animals away, such as an old hamster cage or rabbit run.

Top Tip

You can make a wire container out of chicken wire. It doesn't have to be very big. It is important to make sure no animals can eat the chicken. It will ruin your experiment, and upset their stomachs!

How Do Conditions Affect Rot?

Choose three different conditions to put each chicken thigh in. We put one thigh in foil, one on the soil, and one in a container of water. Be careful to wash your hands really well if you touch the raw meat. It can make you sick.

Predict what you think will happen. Which thigh will rot the quickest? Which will rot the slowest?

Make a log each day, write down the weather, and any changes to the thighs.

	Weather	Water	Soil	Foil
Day 1	80, cloudy	water cloudy	no change	no change
Day 2	71, breeze	smelly	turning green	smelly
Day 14	74, sunny	sludge almost gone	maggots, totally rotted	maggots almost rotted

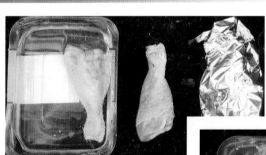

Experiment – Day One

maggots!

Experiment – Day Fourteen

Getting Ready For Court

Part of a forensic pathologist's job is to give evidence in murder **trials**. Detectives have now arrested a suspect in the East Street case. Prisha needs to look back through the notes she made and get ready to give her evidence. A murder trial always takes place many months after she did her autopsy.

Good notes and photographs are important to help her remember all the facts. Prisha usually talks into a **voice recorder** while she is doing an autopsy. Listening back to the recording before the trial really helps her remember all the facts about the case.

Case No: 543

Date: Jan 17 2018

Forensic Pathology Report

Prisha Gupta

East Street Murder

Findings
- The victim suffered a severe head wound
- The victim's nostrils contained traces of soot
- The victim had soil traces in their head wound
- Hair strands were found clasped in the victim's hand

Conclusions
- The cause of death was from a head wound
- The victim inhaled a small amount of smoke just before death
- The soil was found to come from a window box on the second floor balcony

Solve It!

Who do you think is about to stand trial for Sarah-Ann's murder?

a) Sarah-Ann's father, George Proctor?

b) Sarah-Ann's brother, James Proctor?

c) Sarah-Ann's husband, John Preedy?

Answers on page 45

Prisha will have to give her evidence to a **jury** as well as the judge. A jury is a group of members of the public who must decide if the person is guilty or not guilty. They are people from all walks of life, who probably won't have any medical training. Prisha needs to be able to clearly explain any complicated medical details to the jury.

Top Tip

Prisha must tell the facts straight and give the jury all the information they need to make the right decision. She would hate for a guilty person to go free, or an innocent person to go to jail.

The Verdict

Detectives discovered Sarah-Ann's brother, James, had been staying at the apartment on the night she was murdered. Her husband was out of town. Sarah-Ann's brother had lost his job and was struggling to find work. Their parents were quite wealthy. Sarah-Ann refused to give him any money, but was happy to let him stay at her apartment. Detectives also heard the pizza delivery guy was angry. The Preedys had complained about him being late delivering their pizza.

Solve It!

James Proctor was desperate for money. The pizza delivery guy was angry. What do you think happened the night Sarah-Ann Preedy died? The jury will have to decide.

a) James lit a small fire in the hall using last night's pizza box. He woke his sister by banging on her bedroom door. He then hid on the balcony. When she realized she could not leave the flat by the main door she went onto the balcony. James surprised her and pushed her over the railing.

b) The Preedys had ordered a pizza the night before the murder. They had not given the delivery guy a tip, and complained about him being late. The pizza delivery guy was seen on CCTV in the area at 6:00 am. James said he saw the pizza guy put a burning pizza box through the letterbox. James alerted his sister. In her panic she ran onto the dark balcony and fell over the railings.

Answers on page 45

Name: James Proctor

Date of Trial: 01/17/2018
Court No: Court One

Judge Presiding: S Thomlinson

Crime: Murder

Profile: James Proctor was arrested once back in 2013 for being drunk and disorderly. He recently separated from his girlfriend and had lost his job. His girlfriend said he once threatened to kill his sister so that he could inherit all his parents' money. He was living with his sister Sarah-Ann and her husband at the time of the murder.

Prisha gives her evidence in court. The victim's injuries certainly came from a fall from the balcony. Prisha was sure that the time of death was around 5:20 am and not 6:00 am. Detectives had noticed that the balcony was lit all night by streetlights, and would never have been completely dark. The DNA from the hair strands in the victim's hand was matched to her brother, James Proctor.

Now it's up to the jury to decide. What do you think?

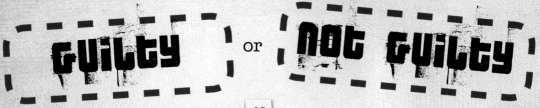

GUILTY or NOT GUILTY

Glossary

analysis A careful study of something to learn about its parts.

autopsy An examination of a dead body especially to find out the cause and manner of death.

botanist A person who specializes in the study of plant life.

coroner An official who holds inquests into violent, sudden, or suspicious deaths.

crime scene The place where an offense has been committed and forensic evidence may be gathered.

CSI Crime scene investigator who collects, preserves and processes evidence at the scene of a crime.

decomposes Breaks down or rots through chemical changes.

dispatched To send away quickly to a particular place or for a particular purpose.

DNA The code in each person's cells that makes everyone unique.

evidence Material presented to a court in a crime case.

hit-and-run A road accident in which the driver who caused the accident drives away without helping the other people involved and without telling the police.

jury A group of people in court who must decide whether someone is guilty or not.

opinion A judgment about a person, a thing, or an event that may not be shared by all.

silt Very small particles of granular material of a size between sand and clay, whose mineral origin is quartz and feldspar.

suicide The act of killing oneself purposely.

suspicious Something likely to arouse suspicion, a feeling that something is wrong without definite evidence.

thermometer An instrument for measuring temperature.

trials Formal examinations of evidence by a judge, typically before a jury, to decide someone's guilt.

victim A person who suffers because of a crime.

voice recorder A device that records sounds so that they can be heard again.

ANSWERS

5 - c, 8 - b, 9 - 1= a, 2 = b, 10 - a, 11 - detective 2 and 4, forensic pathologist 1, 3, and 5, 14 - a, 17 - c, 19 - a, 20 - c, 21 - 1 = b, 2 = c, 3 = a, 23 - 1 drowned, 2 poisoned, 3 stabbed, 24 - 1 heart, 2 brain, 3 lungs, 25 - 1 =b, 2 = a, 3 = d, 4 = c, 5 = e, 6 = f, 29 - 1 = d, 2 = a, 3 = e, 4 = b, 5 = c, 31 - Sarah-Ann's brother, 35 - a (Sarah-Ann didn't smoke), 37 - Solve it = b, Case file = a, 41 - b, 42 - a (the balcony was not dark, the victim was pushed)

WANT TO BE A FORENSIC PATHOLOGIST??

Job: Forensic Pathologist

Job Description: Forensic pathologists are medical professionals with specialist training. Their job is to find out the cause of a death, disease, or injury of a victim. They also estimate the time of death, and the manner of death. They do this by performing examinations and autopsies. Forensic pathologists spend most of their time in the lab, doing autopsies or examining tissue samples under a microscope.

Qualifications needed: It takes years to become a forensic pathologist. At high school budding forensic pathologists should take science subjects such as biology and chemistry. Students must then take a four-year degree in sciences or medical subjects. After they have completed that they must enroll for another four years at medical school, where they usually take some subjects in forensic pathology. The students must then become an M.D. and finally complete another three to four years residency and pass forensic pathology exams.

Employment: Forensic pathologists may work for the city, county or government, or in hospitals, medical schools or private practice.

Further Information

Books

Carmichael, L. E. *Discover Forensic Science*. Minneapolis, MN: Lerner Publications, 2016.

Jeffrey, Gary. *Autopsies: Pathologists at Work (Graphic Forensic Science)*. New York, NY: Rosen Publishers, 2008.

Websites

Learn more about DNA here!
http://learn.genetics.utah.edu/content/basics/dna

Build your own DNA molecule!
http://learn.genetics.utah.edu/content/basics/builddna/

analysis 23
autopsies 12, 22, 30, 35

botany 28

cause of death 12, 40
coroner 5
court 7, 40, 41
crime scene 9, 12, 25, 34,
   35
CSI team 13, 14

databases 27, 30, 32
decomposition 38, 39
detectives 5, 9, 11, 12, 13,
   15, 17, 18, 40, 42
diseases 8
dispatch 4, 5
DNA 30, 31, 32, 33

forensic botany 28
forensics 8

hair 14, 23, 40, 43
hit-and-run 12

identity 10, 11, 16
injuries 14, 25, 40, 43

juries 41

manner of death 37

organs 24, 25

photography 13, 40
pollen 28

seeds 28, 29, 30
soil 14, 17, 25, 26, 30, 40
soil specialists 27

temperature 18, 19, 20, 21
thermal cycler 32
time of death 18, 19, 20, 21

voice recorders 40

witnesses 15, 17

Smoking

Look for these and other books in the Lucent Overview Series:

Abortion
Acid Rain
Adoption
Advertising
Alcoholism
Animal Rights
Artificial Organs
The Beginning of Writing
The Brain
Cancer
Censorship
Child Abuse
Cities
The Collapse of the Soviet Union
Dealing with Death
Death Penalty
Democracy
Drug Abuse
Drugs and Sports
Drug Trafficking
Eating Disorders
Elections
Endangered Species
The End of Apartheid in South Africa
Energy Alternatives
Espionage
Euthanasia
Extraterrestrial Life
Family Violence
Gangs
Garbage
Gay Rights
Genetic Engineering
The Greenhouse Effect
Gun Control
Hate Groups
Hazardous Waste
The Holocaust

Homeless Children
Illegal Immigration
Illiteracy
Immigration
Memory
Mental Illness
Money
Ocean Pollution
Oil Spills
The Olympic Games
Organ Transplants
Ozone
The Palestinian-Israeli Accord
Pesticides
Police Brutality
Population
Prisons
Rainforests
Recycling
The Reunification of Germany
Schools
Smoking
Space Exploration
Special Effects in the Movies
Sports in America
Suicide
Teen Alcoholism
Teen Pregnancy
Teen Sexuality
Teen Suicide
The UFO Challenge
The United Nations
The U.S. Congress
The U.S. Presidency
Vanishing Wetlands
Vietnam
World Hunger
Zoos

Smoking

by David Pietrusza

Library of Congress Cataloging-in-Publication Data

Pietrusza, David, 1949–
    Smoking / by David Pietrusza.
       p. cm. — (Lucent overview series)
    Includes bibliographical references and index.
    Summary: Discusses the history and economic impact of tobacco
smoking and examines such issues as addiction and disease,
smoking and teenagers, and civil rights as related to smoking.
    ISBN 1-56006-186-3
    1. Smoking—United States—Juvenile literature.   2. Tobacco
habit—United States—Juvenile literature.   [1. Smoking.
2. Tobacco habit.]   I. Title. II. Series.
HV5760.P54   1997
362.29'6'0973—dc20   96–35444
                                          CIP
                                          AC

Contents

INTRODUCTION   6

CHAPTER ONE   10
Tobacco: Its History and Economic Impact

CHAPTER TWO   20
Cigarettes and Disease

CHAPTER THREE   34
The Nicotine Debate

CHAPTER FOUR   47
Secondhand Smoke and Smokers' Rights

CHAPTER FIVE   65
Teens and Smoking

CHAPTER SIX   82
Making the Tobacco Companies Pay

ORGANIZATIONS TO CONTACT   97
SUGGESTIONS FOR FURTHER READING   101
WORKS CONSULTED   102
INDEX   107
ABOUT THE AUTHOR   111
PICTURE CREDITS   112

Introduction

MORE THAN 45 MILLION Americans smoke tobacco. Although the percentage of adults who smoke has remained at about 20 percent for several years, the total number of smokers continues to rise as the adult population grows. This trend concerns health professionals, insurance companies, and government agencies because smoking has been linked to many diseases, including lung cancer, heart disease, and emphysema.

The American Lung Association reports that every year more than 430,000 Americans die from the effects of cigarette smoking. Sixteen percent of all preventable deaths are smoking-related. In comparison, only 5 percent of preventable deaths are alcohol-related and just 2 percent result from firearms. "Smoking cuts seventeen years from life expectancy," notes Arlene Vigoda in *USA Today*. "A 30-year-old smoker could expect to live another 34.8 years, compared to 52.7 years for a 30-year-old who had never smoked."

The effects of smoking

According to government studies, smokers are not the only ones who get sick from tobacco smoke. In 1986 the surgeon general's office issued a report about the dangers of secondhand smoke—the smoke nonsmokers inhale around smokers. The report claimed that secondhand smoke caused lung cancer, emphysema, bronchitis, and heart disease. A 1992 Environmental Protection Agency (EPA) report concluded that fifty-three thousand Americans

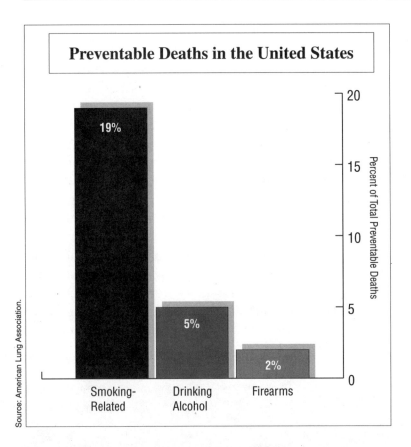

Preventable Deaths in the United States

Smoking-Related: 19%
Drinking Alcohol: 5%
Firearms: 2%

Percent of Total Preventable Deaths

Source: American Lung Association.

die each year from so-called passive smoking. According to the report, a nonsmoker living with a smoker stands a 30 percent greater chance of developing heart disease.

The EPA estimates that tobacco smoke adds $5 to $10 billion annually to building housekeeping and maintenance expenses. These expenses range from damage caused by smoking-related fires to extra maintenance for building ventilation systems, and include the cost of cleaning walls, floors, and ceilings of the residue left by cigarette smoke.

Insurance companies, government agencies, and private businesses, which bear the brunt of these smoking-related costs, have a special interest in limiting the number of people who smoke. For this reason, the private habit of smoking has become a public issue. More and more communities have adopted tougher laws against smoking in public. Only a few years ago people took for granted the license to smoke wherever they wanted—in offices, restaurants, stores, and public buildings. Now public smoking has become relatively rare.

With so much at stake, why do people continue to smoke?

First of all, tobacco producers and millions of consumers reject conclusions that smoking is dangerous. They question much of the research linking smoking to disease, pointing out that millions of smokers never develop cancer or heart disease. They claim that smokers have no more risk of disease than nonsmokers. "[Antismoking propagandists] mislead people that all smokers are at greater risk than nonsmokers," charges pro-smoking activist Carol Thompson. "But excess mortality from all causes, including heart disease and cancer, is concentrated among the minority of people with severe respiratory impairment, and is of similar magnitude regardless of smoking status."

Despite the studies indicating links between smoking, disease, and death, people continue to smoke.

Many smokers feel that laws that constrain their habit are unfair and even unconstitutional. As long as tobacco is a legal product, they argue, current restrictions of its use are at best excessive. In a free society, they maintain, individuals should be allowed to make their own decisions about what products they use and what health risks they take. Supported by such organizations as the Tobacco Institute, a pro-tobacco research and advocacy group, smokers are fighting for their rights.

The current controversies indicate that the debate over smoking is far from ended. Antismoking advocates continue to argue that cigarettes and other tobacco products are unsafe and even deadly. They maintain that tobacco products would never be allowed on the market had they been developed or introduced today. Smokers and the tobacco industry respond that many antitobacco claims have not been proved and that until that time, they should be allowed to exercise their personal and commercial freedom. Only one thing is certain: With millions of lives and billions of dollars at stake, the debate will only heat up.

1

Tobacco: Its History and Economic Impact

CENTURIES BEFORE CHRISTOPHER Columbus sailed to North America, Native Americans discovered that the dried leaves of the tobacco plant produced an aromatic smoke when burned. Unlike the smoke of many other plants, tobacco smoke was not immediately toxic when inhaled. On the contrary, tobacco produced a mild, flavorful smoke. Shredded, placed in wooden or clay pipes, and lit, tobacco gained favor among Native Americans who smoked herbs as a custom and in rituals.

In 1492 two members of Christopher Columbus's crew, Rodrigo de Jerez and Luis de Torres, saw Native Americans in Cuba smoking. De Jerez decided to try the exotic custom himself, enjoyed it, and took some tobacco back to Spain to introduce the practice to his homeland. When de Jerez's highly religious countrymen saw smoke coming out of his nostrils, however, they believed he was possessed by the devil and promptly threw him in jail.

Smoking in the American colonies

Other European visitors to North America also tried the Native American custom and found it pleasing. By 1612 tobacco smoking had become so popular in Europe that the plant became the first cash crop in Great Britain's new North American colonies. Tobacco growing and trading became so lucrative in England's American colonies that George Washington wrote to supporters of American independence in 1776, "If you can't send money, send tobacco."

Some enthusiasts believed that smoking tobacco benefited one's health. William Byrd of Westover, a wealthy Virginia planter and one of the colonies' most prominent diarists, observed:

> I am humbly of opinion, that when there is any danger of pestilence, we can't more effectually consult our preservation than by providing ourselves with a reasonably fresh quantity of fresh, strongly scented tobacco. We should wear it about our clothes and about our coaches. We should hang bundles of it round our bed, and in the apartments wherein we must converse. If we have an aversion to smoking, it would be very prudent to burn some leaves of tobacco in our dining rooms, lest we swallow infection in our meat. It will also be very useful to take snuff plentifully made of the pure leaf to secure the passages of our brain.

The invention of cigarettes

Most early smokers followed the Native American custom of burning the plant in the bowl of a pipe and drawing smoke through the pipe's stem. Some placed shredded tobacco on a whole leaf, then rolled the leaf around the loose tobacco, making a cigar. The smoker lit one end of the cigar, then drew the smoke through the unburned tobacco and into the throat. In the middle of the nineteenth century, a new way of smoking tobacco emerged in the first European nation to witness smoking. Beggars in Spain gathered up discarded cigar butts, removed the unsmoked tobacco, and wrapped it in paper. Smaller than cigars, these new tobacco products became known as cigarettes.

Tobacco companies soon began to make cigarettes from scraps of the leaf left over from cigar production. Less costly than cigars, cigarettes still were not cheap. Like cigars, cigarettes were hand rolled, and even the most skilled worker could make only four cigarettes a minute. American smokers in the 1870s lit up an average of just forty cigarettes a year. That changed in 1881 when the first cigarette-rolling machine was patented. Each new machine

A tobacco planter in colonial Virginia reclines and smokes from a long pipe. Tobacco profits were vital to the colonists, and some believed the plant had health benefits.

could make 120,000 cigarettes a day. Prices fell, and the popularity of cigarettes zoomed.

As more people took up the practice, tobacco companies competed to attract new smokers to their brands through advertising and gimmicks. In the 1880s, for example, the first baseball cards were given away with cigarette purchases. By 1889 more than 73 billion cigarettes had been produced in the United States.

An American institution

During World War I, free cigarettes were handed out to U.S. servicemen to "relax" them while they were in hazardous combat situations. Tobacco soon became identified with patriotism and the war effort against Germany. Thousands of soldiers who had never smoked before were introduced to tobacco from 1914 to 1918.

After the war, cigarettes became identified with another great social cause—women's rights. Before the war, few women smoked, and many were repulsed by the habit. Indeed, America's first antismoking organization was founded by a woman, Lucy Page Gaston. In 1899 Gaston, a former Sunday school teacher, formed the Chicago Anti-Cigarette League, a group that later expanded into the National Anti-Cigarette League. Gaston and her followers believed smoking was immoral and unhealthy. She

A woman operates one of the early cigarette-rolling machines. Mass production of cigarettes in the late 1800s caused their price to fall and their consumption to rise drastically.

described cigarettes as "coffin nails," because she believed they hastened death.

While women pressed for the right to vote, however, many began to smoke. They wanted to show that not all women were prissy do-gooders like Lucy Page Gaston. Women could be risk takers, just like men. Smoking, they believed, emphasized this point because it was a habit condemned as a health risk by the antismoking leagues. As a psychologist employed by the American Tobacco Company observed: "Some women regard cigarettes as symbols of freedom. . . . Cigarettes, which are equated with men, become torches of freedom."

During the Roaring Twenties, physical slimness became more fashionable than it had been in previous decades, and many women, discovering that smoking helped suppress their cravings for food, took up smoking to help control their weight. Tobacco companies were quick to reinforce this belief. Magazine advertisements for Lucky Strike cigarettes urged women to "Reach for a Lucky Instead of a Sweet."

Smoking gains wider popularity

Just as more women were taking up the habit of smoking, an Ohio teenager named Lloyd "Spud" Hughes invented a type of cigarette that gained widespread acceptance among female smokers. Hughes's menthol cigarette produced a more flavorful and soothing smoke than that of traditional cigarettes. Named for its inventor, the first brand of menthol cigarettes, Spuds, proved popular. Other tobacco companies quickly copied Hughes's recipe and began to offer menthol brands of their own. Spurred by these and other factors, annual U.S. cigarette sales, which amounted to 4.4 billion when Lucy Page Gaston founded the Chicago Anti-Cigarette League in 1899, reached 73 billion in 1924, the year she died.

In 1932, Americans elected the first U.S. president widely known to be a smoker. Franklin Delano Roosevelt enjoyed cigarettes, and he was often photographed smoking, with a long-stemmed cigarette holder clenched in his

This 1923 photo shows a young woman lighting a cigarette. By the 1920s, women began to take up smoking both as a symbol of women's rights and as a way to stay slim.

teeth. A victim of polio, Roosevelt moved with the aid of a wheelchair, braces, and crutches, a fact that was downplayed by the media. By contrast, his interest in smoking became an important part of his public image. Smoking made the crippled president appear virile and bold.

President Roosevelt was not the only famous person to be identified with smoking. The cigar was as much a part of the public image of Great Britain's prime minister Winston Churchill as the cigarette was for Roosevelt. American baseball great Babe Ruth was another famous cigar smoker. Comedians Groucho Marx, George Burns, and W. C. Fields made cigars part of their public image, as well. Cigarettes were even more prevalent than cigars among famous artists, entertainers, and athletes of both sexes. Writers Ernest Hemingway, Isak Dinesen, and Albert Camus were famous smokers, as were movie stars Clark Gable, Humphrey Bogart, Marlene Dietrich, and Bette Davis. Cigarette advertising regularly included celebrity endorsements from famous actors such as Ronald Reagan ("No Unpleasant Aftertaste"), entertainers such as Bob Hope and Bing Crosby ("Chesterfield is the best cigarette for you to smoke"), and athletes such as New York Yankees shortstop Phil Rizzuto ("Open 'Em, Smell 'Em, Smoke 'Em").

Government support

When Roosevelt was elected to the first of his four terms, the United States was in the throes of the worst economic downturn in modern history, the Great Depression. Thousands of banks had closed, millions of Americans had lost their jobs, and the economy had all but collapsed. America was still producing crops regularly during the depression, but the market prices were so low that farmers lost money. To aid farmers, Roosevelt's government created agencies and passed legislation to control market prices. Through the Agricultural Adjustment Act (AAA) of 1933 the federal government offered growers a monetary incentive to reduce crop surpluses so that prices for the crops would rise. Though the Supreme Court declared the AAA unconstitutional in 1936, the U.S. Department of Agriculture (USDA) continued to provide farmers with incentives to decrease production in the hope that market prices would increase.

Among its many actions, the USDA created price supports to help stabilize crop prices. Government price supports involve paying farmers a certain amount of money for each acre they farm, whether or not they grow crops on the land. By sometimes paying farmers *not* to grow a crop, the USDA is able to control the quantity of the commodity produced. This allows the government to prevent crop surpluses, which would drive down prices and make it difficult for farmers to earn a profit. Like other farmers, tobacco farmers began to receive price supports in the 1930s.

The Agriculture Department also developed the policy of extending low-interest loans to farmers in the event that prices fall too low for farmers to operate at a profit. Instead of selling their crop to the tobacco companies, farmers stockpile it to sell when prices are higher. Only then do they repay the loan to the USDA. Even though tobacco is one of the most profitable of all crops, tobacco farmers have received such loans for more than sixty years. With

Actors like Clark Gable, pictured here with a pipe, were often associated with smoking. Many celebrities in the 1930s, including comedians, athletes, writers, and entertainers, endorsed smoking.

the help of the government and the growing demand for cigarettes, tobacco has remained one of America's leading cash crops.

Since the 1930s, smoking has been linked to numerous diseases, prompting the federal government to issue warnings about the dangers of cigarette smoking. In fact, one federal agency—the Office on Smoking and Health (OSH)—was created by Congress for the sole purpose of educating the public about the consequences of smoking. Since 1980, OSH has spent more than $20 million of the taxpayers' money to discourage smoking. Meanwhile, another federal agency—the USDA—has spent $15 million a year to administer the price support program. Many government leaders find this contradiction confusing, if not hypocritical. "We're telling everybody tobacco is dangerous and will kill you," comments Representative Dick Durbin, a Democrat from Illinois, "yet the government is subsidizing it. This defies any kind of rational behavior."

Tobacco industry contributions

Some critics of the tobacco industry disagree with Durbin; they believe the behavior of Congress is completely rational, considering the vast sums of money that the tobacco industry contributes to political campaigns. Common Cause, a political watchdog group, reported that between 1985 and 1995 the tobacco industry gave more than $10.6 million to candidates for federal office, to political action committees (PACs), and to political party committees. "They're giving such large amounts of money it's hard to believe they don't expect something in return," says Representative Henry Waxman, a Democrat from California. Former U.S. surgeon general C. Everett Koop agrees: "The support of politicians and political parties by those associated with tobacco interests is unconscionable. How can Americans believe political promises for health care reform when both parties seem to be associated with an industry that disseminates disease, disability, and death?"

Supporters of the tobacco industry believe that price supports and loans to tobacco farmers remain a wise investment. They argue that the tobacco industry generates billions of dollars in taxes for federal, state, and local governments. The tobacco companies themselves pay millions of dollars in taxes, as do the hundreds of thousands of workers who are directly and indirectly employed by the tobacco industry. The trucking companies that haul tobacco products across the country pay millions of dollars more in fuel taxes. The consumers of tobacco products also pay an astonishing amount in taxes to enjoy their habit. One state, Michigan, derived $245 million in excise tax revenues and another $60 million in general sales taxes from the sale of cigarettes in 1992 alone.

Even when a politician acts to discourage smoking, the result can inadvertently aid the tobacco industry. For example, when President Bill Clinton proposed levying a two-dollar federal excise tax on every pack of cigarettes sold, a tobacco company executive responded calmly. "You know, I don't really care about the excise tax at all," the executive told Roger Rosenblatt of the *New York Times Magazine*. "I wouldn't mind making the Government a little more dependent on the habit."

2

Cigarettes and Disease

AS SMOKING ACHIEVED widespread acceptance during the 1930s, a physician observed something strange that he believed might be related to the popular habit. A patient came to Dr. Alton Ochsner in 1936 exhibiting all the signs of lung cancer. Dr. Ochsner had not seen a single case of this dreaded disease since he was a medical student at St. Louis's Barnes Hospital seventeen years earlier. At that time, Ochsner and other physicians-in-training were hurriedly called to the autopsy of a patient who had died of lung cancer because, as Ochsner's professor put it, the disease was so rare that they probably would never witness another example of it in their entire careers. Ochsner's professor was wrong, however. The patient Ochsner examined in 1936 clearly suffered from lung cancer, as did another patient who came to him a few weeks later. Soon another lung cancer patient showed up, then another, and another. "In a period of six months, I saw nine patients with cancer of the lung," he later wrote. "This represents an epidemic for which there had to be a cause."

Dr. Ochsner carefully interviewed his patients about all aspects of their lives—their jobs, their habits, other illnesses they had experienced. The nine men came from different walks of life and had diverse medical histories. They did have one thing in common, however. "All the afflicted patients were men who smoked heavily and had smoked since World War I," Ochsner noted.

Had Lucy Gaston and other anti-smoking activists been right to call cigarettes "coffin nails"? Was there a connection between smoking and lung cancer? Ochsner believed so, and he was not alone in his belief.

The rise of lung cancer

In 1932 an article appeared in the *American Journal of Cancer* linking tar, one of the forty-seven hundred different chemical compounds found in a tobacco leaf, with the rise in lung cancer. The article supported what a few scattered doctors had begun to suspect, but the report appeared during the depression, when there was little money to fund additional research. The American economic recovery coincided with its entry in World War II against the Axis powers of Germany, Japan, and Italy, and lung cancer research was again deferred. Indeed, President Roosevelt declared that tobacco growing was essential to defeating America's enemies, since smoking would "relax" soldiers and sailors in stressful situations. Throughout World War II, cigarettes were offered at cost or free to U.S. servicemen. As in World War I, hundreds of thousands of nonsmokers were introduced to smoking while serving their country in and out of uniform.

During and after the war, the number of lung cancer cases continued to grow. In 1930 there were only 5 cases of lung cancer among 100,000 males in the U.S. population. By 1950 that number had increased fourfold, to 20 cases per 100,000. And the correlation held for women, too. In the early part of the century relatively few women smoked. Each decade saw further increases, however, and as the number of women smokers grew, so did the incidence of lung cancer among women.

The next major study of the relationship between smoking and lung cancer was published in 1950. Evarts A.

Dr. Alton Ochsner began to suspect an association between smoking and lung cancer in 1936, when the then relatively rare disease developed among several heavy smokers.

Graham, a prominent St. Louis surgeon, and Ernst Wynder, a medical student, wrote an article that appeared in the *Journal of the American Medical Association (JAMA)* stating that practically all study participants with lung cancer had been heavy smokers. Graham and Wynder did not explain how smoking caused lung cancer. They simply inferred from the statistics that smoking and cancer were somehow linked. Like thousands of physicians, Graham was himself a heavy smoker. After completing his research he quit smoking, but he died of lung cancer the following year.

Unlike the 1930 study linking smoking and lung cancer, Graham and Wynder's findings inspired a great deal of follow-up research. Studies of smoking and cancer continued through the 1950s. In 1959 Surgeon General Leroy E. Burney published an article in *JAMA* stating that cigarette smoking caused cancer. In 1962 President John F. Kennedy assigned his surgeon general, Luther Terry, to conduct an extensive study of the issue. Kennedy was assassinated before Terry finished his study, but in January 1964 Terry reported that smoking was a major cause of lung cancer in men. Terry also found that smoking contributed to many other lung diseases.

Bronchitis

Lung cancer is the most widely recognized lung disease linked to smoking, but it is not the only one. Scientific studies have also associated two types of bronchitis—acute bronchitis and chronic bronchitis—with smoking, although these diseases can also be caused by prolonged exposure to dust and industrial pollution. Like dust and pollution, tobacco smoke irritates the membranes lining the bronchial tubes, the air passages that bring air into the lungs. This irritation causes the tubes to constrict. The same thing happens to the bronchioli, the smaller branches of the bronchial tubes that funnel air into even smaller ducts within the lungs. The irritation of the bronchial tubes and the bronchioli triggers the creation of mucus. As a result, a person with bronchitis coughs heavily and often expectorates large amounts of mucus. A fairly brief, more or less severe episode is called acute bronchitis; repeated episodes triggered by continual irritation can lead to its chronic form. Smokers face a fivefold greater risk of dying from acute bronchitis than do nonsmokers. There is no cure for chronic bronchitis.

Emphysema

Smoking has also been linked to another serious lung disease, emphysema. Like bronchitis, emphysema inhibits breathing. Instead of restricting the passage of air through the bronchial tubes and bronchioli as bronchitis does, emphysema cuts down on the ability of the small air sacs found in the lungs, the alveoli, to function. Normally, the alveoli make possible the exchange of oxygen and carbon dioxide within the lungs and help keep open the bronchial tubes. This exchange is even more vital to a smoker than to a nonsmoker, since 4 percent of all cigarette smoke is composed of carbon monoxide, a gas which taken in large dosages can be fatal. Large amounts of carbon monoxide in the bloodstream make it difficult to transport oxygen to the body's organs, and cells deprived of oxygen die.

Emphysema breaks down the alveoli's walls, ultimately destroying them. The exchange of oxygen and carbon dioxide can no longer take place, and the bronchial tubes are no longer held open. Not only is too little air taken into the lungs, but the air that is taken in cannot properly give up its oxygen and take on carbon dioxide to be expelled. A chronic shortness of breath results, and an emphysema victim often is incapable of the slightest exertion. Some are forced to use artificial respirators to enable them to breath. Many emphysema patients die from infections that result from the disease, from respiratory failure, or from heart disease. As in the case of acute bronchitis, smokers face a fivefold greater risk of dying from emphysema than do nonsmokers.

Smoking and pregnancy

An unborn child receives all of its oxygen from its mother, so it is not surprising that an unborn child can be

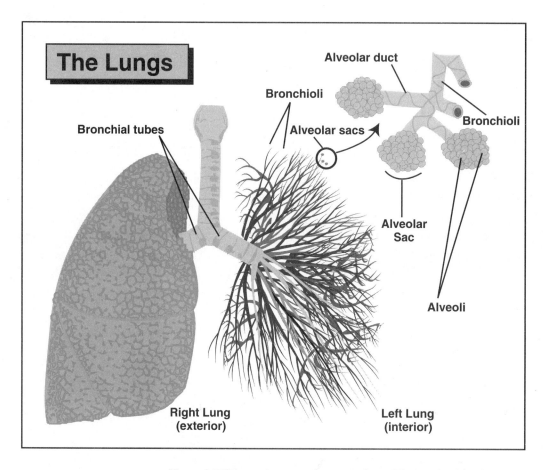

The Lungs

Bronchial tubes

Bronchioli

Alveolar sacs

Alveolar duct

Bronchioli

Alveolar Sac

Alveoli

Right Lung
(exterior)

Left Lung
(interior)

This diagram of the lungs shows the areas affected by smoking-related diseases. Bronchitis irritates the bronchial tubes and bronchioli, creating mucus, and emphysema destroys the alveoli, shown in the close-up.

affected if his or her mother smokes. Through the placenta (an organ that connects the fetus to the mother), unborn babies actually absorb the nicotine, carbon monoxide, and tar that the mother has inhaled while smoking. Ingesting carbon monoxide prevents the baby from receiving the oxygen and nutrients it needs for proper development. Studies have shown that 25 percent of the normal flow of oxygen to the fetus is cut off by a mother's smoking.

Smoking's interference with the normal oxygen flow to the fetus causes a wide variety of health problems. The lack of oxygen may affect the development of the brain; studies of three- and four-year-olds whose mothers smoked during pregnancy have revealed they have lower IQs than a control group whose mothers did not smoke. It is estimated that smoking causes 20 to 30 percent of all low-birth-weight births in the United States and as much as 14 percent of all premature deliveries. It causes a full 10 percent of infant deaths. Smoking during pregnancy has also been linked to asthma in infancy.

Scientists have found that the best way to prevent such problems is for pregnant women to avoid smoking altogether. Switching to low-tar cigarettes or simply reducing smoking seems to have little effect; only quitting entirely seems to make a difference.

Heart disease

Because the lungs of a smoker are exposed to toxic chemicals with each puff of a cigarette, cigar, or pipe, these vital organs are the most directly affected by smoking. As in the case of an expectant mother who smokes, however, problems in the lungs can cause problems elsewhere in the

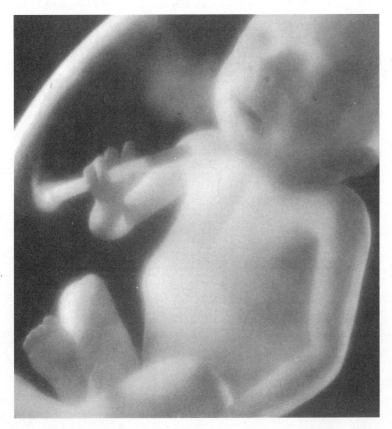

This image from an American Cancer Society ad features a fetus holding a cigarette and is meant to discourage pregnant women from smoking. A pregnant smoker's child actually ingests the nicotine, tar, and carbon monoxide through the placenta.

body. For example, smoking makes it much more difficult for the heart to operate. One chemical in tobacco smoke, a substance known as nicotine, constricts the blood vessels. As a result, the heart must work harder to pump blood through the body. Over a long period of time, this added exertion can seriously weaken the heart.

Like all the organs of the body, the heart needs oxygen to stay healthy. Smoking, however, increases the amount of carbon monoxide in the bloodstream, leaving less room for oxygen. The decreased amount of oxygen in the bloodstream damages the heart. Carbon monoxide in the bloodstream also causes cholesterol to build up in a person's arteries. When that happens, the flow of blood leading to the heart is choked off, causing a heart attack.

AGE clogs arteries

In May 1996 researchers from the Pickower Institute of Manhasset, New York, released the results of a study indicating that smoking releases a sort of "molecular glue" called advanced glucation endproducts, or AGE, that clogs arteries and contributes to heart disease. AGE may also cause circulatory problems and even cataracts (the clouding of an eye's lens or of its surrounding transparent membrane that obstructs the passage of light). The Pickower Institute found increased AGE levels in smokers' blood. It also discovered that exposing laboratory rats to cigarette smoke for just twenty-two hours resulted in a 75 percent increase in their AGE levels. Since both rats and humans are mammals and have somewhat analogous physical systems, some researchers feel humans' AGE levels have been raised by cigarette smoke, just as the rats' were.

Other researchers, however, caution against placing too much importance on these findings. "Ten years from now," Dr. David Meyerson, a cardiologist at Johns Hopkins University, comments, "it may turn out to be a landmark work—and it may not."

Regardless of how important increased levels of AGE prove to be, the fact remains that smoking has been shown to increase heart disease. In fact, 191,000 people in

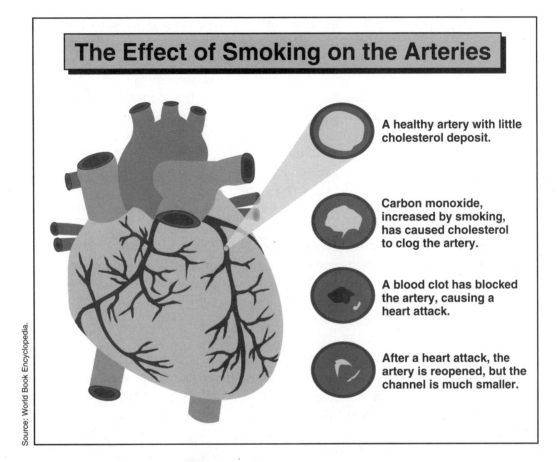

The Effect of Smoking on the Arteries

A healthy artery with little cholesterol deposit.

Carbon monoxide, increased by smoking, has caused cholesterol to clog the artery.

A blood clot has blocked the artery, causing a heart attack.

After a heart attack, the artery is reopened, but the channel is much smaller.

Source: World Book Encyclopedia.

the United States die each year from smoking-related heart disease—far more than die from lung cancer.

Other smoking-related diseases

Decreased levels of oxygen in the blood affect not just the heart, but nearly all the organs of the body. Recent studies have also revealed that cigarette smoke can cause cataracts, the leading cause of blindness worldwide. More than 50 million people suffer from cataracts worldwide, including 3 million Americans. Study results published in *JAMA* reveal that 20 percent of all cataracts may be caused by smoking. The study monitored the smoking habits of approximately eighteen thousand male physicians and more than fifty thousand female nurses. It found that among the males, a smoker had nearly a 50 percent greater chance of developing cataracts; women had a 60 percent greater chance of having cataracts.

A two-year study by Tufts University researchers, completed in 1991, found that smoking may play a significant role in osteoporosis, a disease that decreases bone mass and enlarges space between bone cells, producing very porous and fragile bones. Osteoporosis results in 1.5 million bone fractures and 300,000 hip fractures each year. Nearly 25 million people suffer from the disease, most of whom are elderly women. The Tufts study of post-menopausal women, published in the *Journal of Bone and Mineral Research*, indicates that smokers lost 1 percent of their bone mass each year. Women who did not smoke lost virtually none of their bone mass. The study guessed that smoking may block the intestines' ability to absorb calcium. Another two-year study, conducted by Richard Mazess of the University of Wisconsin, Madison, found a connection between cigarette smoking and the weak bones of Caucasian women between the ages of twenty and thirty-nine. "Osteoporosis is probably the least of the reasons women shouldn't smoke," said Mazess, "but it's worth noting."

A serious warning

The various findings about the dangers of smoking have been widely reported in the media and by the government. For example, when Surgeon General Luther Terry concluded in 1964 that smoking caused lung cancer, he urged Congress to enact a law that would require tobacco companies to print a warning on cigarette packages. The 1964 *Surgeon General's Report on Smoking and Tobacco* stated, "The risk of developing lung cancer increases with the duration of smoking and the number of cigarettes smoked per day and is diminished by discontinuing smoking." The surgeon general's report also linked smoking to emphysema. Although the tobacco industry disputed Terry's findings, Congress decided to follow the surgeon general's recommendation. In 1966 the federal government mandated that each cigarette pack carry a label warning "Caution—cigarette smoking may be hazardous to your health."

Many scientists did not believe the warning was worded strongly enough, and they went about the task of trying to prove a stronger link between smoking and various illnesses. In 1967 the surgeon general linked smoking to heart disease. In 1978, Congress altered the surgeon general's warning label to read, "Smoking is known to cause cancer and other diseases."

Despite these warnings and the nearly continuous outpouring of research that condemned smoking, however, millions of Americans continued to smoke. Some doubted the scientific findings and took comfort in the tobacco companies' insistence that science had not proved conclusively that smoking was the sole cause of the illnesses

Surgeon General Luther Terry displays a report on smoking and health. Dr. Terry found smoking to cause lung cancer and recommended that cigarette packs carry warning labels.

attributed to it. After all, many people smoked into old age and never got sick. Smokers who live long and healthy lives sometimes attribute their vitality to the pleasure they receive from cigarettes.

Pro-smoking advocates dispute much of the statistical research that blames smoking for disease. For one thing, they point out that showing a relationship between a particular behavior and a disease is not the same thing as showing that the behavior causes the disease. Indeed, scientists have not fully explained how certain chemicals in tobacco actually cause changes in human health.

Looking for a connection

Many of the studies that have tried to show a causal, rather than correlative, relationship between smoking and disease have involved experiments on animals. Some scientists question the value of these studies as well, pointing out that animals may react differently to a particular chemical than a person would. In addition, the dosages of chemicals that are given to laboratory animals often ex-

Cigarette packs now bear variations of the warning labels initiated by Surgeon General Terry in 1964. The tobacco industry argued that his findings were inconclusive and many people continued to smoke.

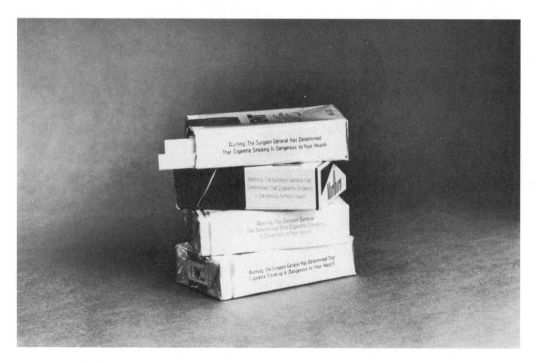

ceed the amount of the chemical a person is likely to encounter in a lifetime, and sometimes in two, three, or more lifetimes. "Mice have been painted, hamsters swabbed, and rats injected with 'tars' condensed from tobacco smoke in laboratories but not found in smoke," writes Horace R. Kornegay, an attorney and a former president of the Tobacco Institute. "Subsequent changes in various cells of these animals have been cited as evidence that cigarettes cause diseases, though production with smoke of human-type lung cancer—or heart disease or emphysema—has *never been verified* in laboratory experiments."

Biased studies

Critics also question the methods used in statistical studies that allegedly prove links between smoking and disease. A study released in Hawaii in 1991 alleged that those studies linking smoking and heart disease were biased. According to its authors, antismoking researchers had ignored evidence that factors other than smoking were far more significant causes of heart disease. A Danish study supported these findings. The Copenhagen Male Study followed the health of 4,710 Danish men for seventeen years. Researchers found no difference in heart disease rates between smokers and nonsmokers. Writes B. Bruce-Biggs in *Fortune* magazine:

> Although the Public Health Service has been reticent about publishing the fact, every study cited in support of the statement that "cigarette smoking causes cancer" reveals that a smoker is unlikely to get cancer—only that he is statistically more likely to get it than a non-smoker. No one can say how much more likely. This is true of all supposed carcinogens.

Many smokers do not question the findings that link smoking and disease, but refuse to believe that they personally will be struck by a smoking-related disease. Other smokers are fatalistic. Everyone dies from something, they reason, so what does it matter if they die from a smoking-related disease or from some other disease or mishap? In the meantime, they enjoy their remaining time by continuing to smoke.

This lung cancer patient is on a respirator. Although evidence indicated a link between smoking and lung cancer, smoking advocates claimed that the studies proved nothing.

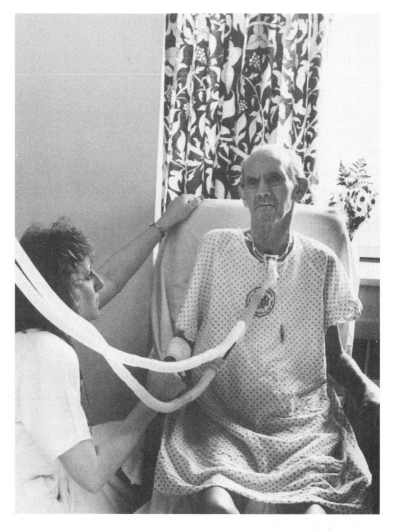

Some nonsmokers are amazed by the loyalty smokers show to their habit. "In the history of the universe," noted William Ecenbarger in an April 1992 *Reader's Digest* article, "there has never been a greater discrepancy between knowledge and behavior."

Was smoking addictive?

For some time, others were not so sure that the behavior of smokers was entirely a matter of free choice. They suspected that something more was behind the allegiance to tobacco than great taste, great advertising, or philosophical beliefs. These doubts were especially strong among those who had once smoked and tried to quit. Almost all smokers found that when they gave up the habit, they missed the activity of smoking: the smell of smoke, the feel of a cigarette in their hand, the very act of lighting up. Many also found that soon after they quit smoking they experienced physical reactions such as headaches, sweating, and shaking. Eventually these symptoms would go away, but sometimes the physical craving for tobacco overcame the desire to quit. The temporary nature of these symptoms and the fact that they appeared soon after a person gave up smoking caused many people to conclude that smokers were experiencing withdrawal symptoms similar to those experienced by drug addicts. Were smokers addicted to tobacco? For many, the answer was obvious: Yes.

3

The Nicotine Debate

GIVING UP ANY habit can be difficult, but giving up smoking is especially difficult. Some scientists believe the reason for this lies deep within the tobacco leaf, in a chemical known as nicotine. An oily alkaloid that is found only in tobacco, nicotine turns brown when it is exposed to the air. It is extremely poisonous. Just two or three drops (50 milligrams) of pure nicotine on a person's tongue results in a quick death. The substance paralyzes the autonomic nervous system, causing convulsions, respiratory failure, and general loss of mobility. Nicotine is such an effective killer that it is used by farmers and gardeners as an insecticide.

The average cigarette today contains 12 to 18 milligrams of nicotine. In the 1950s, cigarettes contained as much as 75 percent more than that. However, because the nicotine found in cigarette smoke is not in a pure state it does not prove fatal to smokers. Only about 1 milligram is absorbed into a normal smoker's bloodstream with each cigarette.

Once nicotine smoke reaches the lungs' alveoli it is very quickly absorbed into the bloodstream, often in as little as seven seconds. The blood then carries it to the brain. Nicotine inhaled in cigarette smoke reaches the brain more quickly than heroin injected into the veins with a needle.

At first smokers usually react very negatively to nicotine. Quite often first-time smokers experience an extremely harsh physical reaction. Some have headaches and dizziness. Others become nauseated and even vomit. Eventually, though, smokers can become more tolerant of

Extinguishing a single cigarette may be easy, but for many people the addictive substances in cigarettes, like nicotine, make it difficult to quit completely.

nicotine. The body learns to accept the substance and these unpleasant reactions disappear.

Addiction

But the body does more than just "accept" nicotine. It learns to crave it. Scientists widely believe that it is nicotine that causes smoking to be habit-forming. Smokers must inhale greater and greater quantities of nicotine to quiet their craving for it. "Smokers often find they need a second cigarette—and another and another—in order to get the same feelings," states the American Lung Association. "After a while, they find the number of cigarettes that keeps them satisfied. At that point, the person is physically addicted and will only feel comfortable when nicotine is in his or her system." An eight-member advisory panel for the Food and Drug Administration (FDA) agreed. In a report issued in August 1994 the panel concluded that "the amount of nicotine delivered by currently marketed cigarettes [is] likely to lead to addiction in the typical smoker."

The tobacco industry disputes the notion that smoking is addictive. "I do not believe nicotine is addictive," Thomas Sandefur, chairman and CEO of Brown & Williamson, told a congressional subcommittee in 1994. "Nicotine is a very important constituent in the cigarette smoke for taste." Supporting the tobacco industry's contention is the fact that millions of smokers actually *have* quit smoking. This fact raises a question: If so many have quit, how can smoking be addictive? "To some people, smoking is addictive," presidential candidate Bob Dole commented in June 1996. "To others, they can take it or leave it."

Many scientists agree that nicotine is not addictive. Among them is Dominec Ciraulo of the Tufts University School of Medicine, who points out that nicotine does not produce the sort of intoxication or "buzz" that such addictive substances as opiates do. Therefore, Ciraulo reasons, nicotine cannot and should not be considered addictive.

Acetaldehyde studies

Not all of cigarettes' habit-forming qualities may actually result from nicotine. A little-known by-product of tobacco smoke called acetaldehyde may also be to blame. In 1994 a former tobacco company researcher revealed to a congressional committee that he had studied acetaldehyde and found it to be as addictive or "reinforcing" in animals as nicotine. When the two substances were found together, as they are in cigarette smoke, the result was a doubly strong source of addiction.

The researcher's experimental subjects were rats that were placed in a cage with a lever they could operate. The lever was designed to release four different substances: saltwater, saltwater containing nicotine, saltwater containing acetaldehyde, and saltwater containing a mixture of nicotine and acetaldehyde. When the lever released plain saltwater, the rats used it just 8 times each day. When it released nicotine, the rats used it 90 times a day. When it released acetaldehyde, they used it 240 times a day. When it released a mixture of nicotine and acetaldehyde, the rats used it 400 times each day. The researchers concluded that combining nicotine and acetaldehyde significantly magnifies their separate addictive potential in rats—and would do so in humans as well.

Just as horticulturists have developed different varieties of corn, squash, roses, and many other plants, they have also developed different varieties of the tobacco plant. When smoked, the leaves of these different tobacco plants produce different flavors. Connoisseurs of tobacco combine leaves of different strains to create a blend that tastes especially good. American tobacco companies have created some of their most popular brands by blending domestic tobacco with imported Turkish and Greek leaf.

Tobacco leaves, like these, come in a variety of types, and each one has a different amount of nicotine. Nicotine levels also vary in different parts of the plant.

The amount of nicotine in a tobacco leaf varies from one type of plant to another. The three main types of tobacco—bright, burley, and oriental—each have unique levels of nicotine. In addition, leaves higher on the stalk of the tobacco plant contain more nicotine than leaves lower

on the stalk. Ribs and stems of leaves contain less than the rest of the leaf. Taking these factors into account, tobacco companies can control the amount of nicotine in a specific blend—a fact they freely admit, since they regard nicotine as an important flavor component.

Controlling the amount of nicotine

Antismoking advocates reject the claim that the only reason tobacco companies blend various parts of the stalks and different varieties of tobacco is to create a pleasant taste for their product. These critics contend that the companies manipulate the amount of nicotine in cigarettes to sustain the addictive properties of cigarettes and keep smokers hooked. Some of the evidence for this conclusion has come from inside the tobacco industry itself, from internal memos that acknowledge quite frankly the function of nicotine in cigarettes. For example, in the early 1960s, when many tranquilizers were just coming on the market, cigarette executives worried about this new form of competition, since cigarettes were widely believed to be highly

relaxing. "We are," wrote Brown & Williamson's chief counsel to other company executives, "in the business of selling nicotine, an addictive drug effective in the release of stress mechanisms."

The FDA has strongly hinted that tobacco companies manipulate the amount of nicotine found in cigarettes. In February 1994 FDA commissioner David Kessler wrote to the Coalition on Smoking and Health, an alliance of groups that oppose smoking, "Although technology was developed years ago to remove nicotine from cigarettes and to control with precision the amount of nicotine in cigarettes, [they] are still marketed with levels of nicotine that are sufficient to produce and sustain addiction."

Denied allegations

Kessler also reported information (often internal tobacco industry correspondence) he was receiving regarding alleged cigarette manufacturer manipulation of nicotine levels.

> Evidence brought to our attention is accumulating that suggests that cigarette manufacturers may intend that their products contain nicotine to satisfy an addiction on the part of some of their customers. In fact, it is our understanding that manufacturers commonly add nicotine to cigarettes to deliver specific amounts of nicotine.

Kessler revealed that Brown & Williamson had developed a variety of tobacco, called Y-1, that contained nearly double the normal amount of nicotine. According to Kessler, Brown & Williamson had imported nearly four million pounds of Y-1 leaf into the United States by 1994.

The company denied any intent to raise nicotine levels, saying it was instead merely trying to maintain natural nicotine levels. It charged the FDA and antismoking advocates with trying to create an unfavorable impression of tobacco companies to further turn public opinion against their industry.

"There is no manipulation in the way that they are trying to characterize it," says the Tobacco Institute's

This antismoking demonstration depicts the Statue of Liberty chained by smoking. The tobacco industry has been accused of manipulating the nicotine levels in cigarettes to keep smokers addicted, or chained, to their habits.

Brennan Dawson. "They are using the word 'manipulate' with a sinister characterization."

"A vehicle for delivering nicotine"

While tobacco company executives denied that they manipulated the amount of nicotine in cigarettes to create a dependency or addiction, antismoking advocates continued to search for a "smoking gun," solid proof that the tobacco companies were lying about smoking, nicotine, and addiction. In October 1995 the activists believed they had finally found such proof. It came in the form of an internal tobacco industry memo mailed anonymously to the FDA by someone calling himself "a concerned citizen" who "cannot sign my name because it would place my family at risk." Written by a former R. J. Reynolds executive in 1972, the memo seemed to admit things about the link between tobacco and nicotine that the tobacco companies had long denied.

The author of the memo was Claude Teague, RJR's assistant research director. Teague wrote that smokers chose a cigarette brand mainly because of "individual nicotine dosage requirements and [only] secondarily by a variety of other considerations, including flavor." He continued, "A tobacco product is, in essence, a vehicle for delivering nicotine. Happily for the tobacco industry, nicotine is both habituating [habit-forming] and unique in its variety of physiological actions."

Informed of the discovery, Peggy Carter, a spokesperson for R. J. Reynolds, stated that the memo did not reflect the company's beliefs on the subject. The company was not in the business of addicting people to its products, Carter said. Claude Teague's memo was merely one employee's opinion—and not even an accurate one, for that matter. "Do people," said Carter, "sometimes in their musings say things that may not be reflective of the company's position? Yes."

Another internal memo

Yet Claude Teague's memo was not the only embarrassing document to surface in 1995. In December a similar tobacco company internal memorandum appeared, this time from within the Philip Morris Companies. The memo was undated, but it could not have been written before 1992. That meant the memo was written at a time when the addictive properties of nicotine were well known. Again, cigarettes were called "nicotine delivery systems." Again, the company in question denied the document reflected company policy. But Victor Noble, a former Philip Morris researcher, claimed that the memorandum was evidence that "what these tobacco companies say publicly is very, very different from what they say internally. . . . Internally they view cigarettes as a nice delivery vehicle and nicotine as a drug. Publicly, they say nicotine is a flavor molecule."

Critics of the tobacco industry were especially interested in the discussions taking place among tobacco company executives about the nature of nicotine. If the tobacco industry believed that nicotine was addictive, it would bolster the assertion of antismoking advocates that nicotine is a drug. The distinction was not just semantic. If nicotine were a drug, cigarettes would be subject to strict regulation by the one power that could change forever the way tobacco companies do business—the U.S. government.

Government regulation

Ever since Rodrigo de Jerez was thrown into a Spanish jail for smoking in 1493, opponents of smoking have used the power of government to restrict, regulate, discourage, and even prohibit smoking. Believing that smoking was both unsafe and immoral, antismoking advocates in the United States convinced the legislatures of North Dakota, Iowa, and Tennessee to ban the sale and use of cigarettes in 1887. The antismoking movement quickly spread to

other states. By the 1890s, cigarette smoking was prohibited in twenty-six states.

Many people considered smoking to be a "gateway" activity, a bad habit that frequently led to even worse ones. "The relationship of tobacco," noted one magazine article in 1912, "especially in the form of cigarettes, and alcohol and opium is a very close one. . . . Morphine is the legitimate consequence of alcohol, and alcohol is the legitimate consequence of tobacco."

When the U.S. government began to provide cigarettes to soldiers fighting in World War I, the opponents of smoking began to lose ground. Smoking became so linked to the war effort in many people's minds that those who campaigned against smoking were accused of lack of patriotism. Prosecutors in Indiana actually indicted several antismoking activists for treason.

One by one, state legislatures across the United States began to reconsider their antismoking laws. By 1921, five states had lifted their bans against cigarettes, and by 1930 the prohibition against smoking had come to an end in all the states that had banned the habit.

Tobacco taxes

As public support for smoking bans began to erode, the opponents of smoking changed their tactics. If smoking could not be outlawed, at least it could be taxed. If taxes on tobacco products were high enough, the antismoking advocates reasoned, people would be discouraged from pursuing the habit.

A tax imposed by the government to discourage people from doing something legal but immoral is known as a sin tax. In addition to discouraging an undesirable behavior, sin taxes also raise large amounts of money for state and federal governments. Iowa, in 1921, was the first state to levy a sin tax on cigarettes. By 1948 thirty-six states were raising $340 million yearly from such taxes. By the 1990s smokers were annually paying $11 billion in federal and state taxes. Counting state taxes, smokers pay an average of 56 cents in taxes on each pack of cigarettes they buy today.

A soldier lights a cigarette while in his foxhole. The prevalence of servicemen's smoking during World War I and World War II paved the way for increased public acceptance of the habit.

When the surgeon general's office published the *Surgeon General's Report on Smoking and Tobacco* in 1964, antismoking advocates urged the government to do more to discourage smoking. The warning label mandated by Congress in 1966 was a start, but the antismoking lobby urged stronger action. Believing that what Americans heard and saw contributed to their interest in smoking, the federal government banned all tobacco advertising (except for smokeless tobacco) on radio and television in 1971.

Classifying nicotine as a drug

As evidence about the addictive power of nicotine began to mount in the 1980s and 1990s, some antismoking activists called upon the federal government to more tightly control the tobacco industry. They argued that nicotine was a drug and therefore was subject to regulation by the U.S. Food and Drug Administration, the federal agency responsible for ensuring that foods are pure and that drugs are safe and effective. Many officials within the FDA agreed, arguing that the agency has the right to control any substance that could "affect a structure or

Workers erect a giant cigarette advertisement stating, "The choice is taste." Tobacco companies claim that nicotine is used as a flavor enhancer, not as a means of maintaining addiction.

function of the [human] body"—a definition that would apply to cigarettes and nicotine.

The FDA had never before regulated tobacco products. Tobacco was not a food, and previously it had not been considered a drug. If, however, the FDA took responsibility for regulating tobacco products, cigarettes could be subject to all sorts of government restrictions: federal rules on sales to minors, stricter advertising and promotional regulations, controls on what sort of tobacco was used to make cigarettes, limits on how much tar and nicotine a cigarette could contain. The FDA might even try to ban cigarettes altogether.

This is why tobacco industry executives were so disturbed when FDA commissioner David Kessler said that cigarettes "contain nicotine to satisfy an addiction." A spokesperson for Philip Morris USA voiced a growing suspicion within the tobacco industry that Kessler "apparently has a secret plan to impose more and more government regulation from Washington—regulations that . . . strike at the heart of the right of adults to make decisions for themselves." The tobacco industry challenged the FDA's contention that cigarettes are a delivery system for an addictive substance, saying that based on the FDA's definitions of addiction, the average person could not tell the difference between the addiction allegedly caused by cigarettes and the addiction caused by crack cocaine. The tobacco industry knows that if the FDA gains the authority to regulate cigarettes, it will threaten not only the industry's profitability, but its very existence.

4

Secondhand Smoke and Smokers' Rights

THE FDA IS NOT the only government agency to pose a threat to the health of the tobacco industry. In December 1992 another federal agency, the Environmental Protection Agency, issued a report that had an immediate effect on smoking. *Respiratory Health Effects of Passive Smoking: Lung Cancer and Other Disorders* claimed that cigarette smoke causes 3,000 deaths from lung cancer, 13,000 deaths from other cancers, and 37,000 deaths from lung disease in the United States each year. What was surprising was that the victims of these diseases are not smokers themselves. They do not become ill and die from what is known as mainstream smoke, the type of smoke drawn through a cigarette and inhaled directly into a smoker's lungs. They are killed by secondhand smoke.

ETS

The scientific term for secondhand smoke is environmental tobacco smoke (ETS). ETS is made up of two kinds of tobacco smoke. Most ETS (85 to 90 percent) is sidestream smoke, the kind of smoke that is released by the burning tobacco between puffs. The remaining 10 to 15 percent of ETS is smoke that is exhaled by a smoker.

The EPA found that while ETS clearly is not as toxic as mainstream smoke, it is nonetheless a dangerous substance.

Of the more than 4,000 chemical compounds in second-hand smoke, an estimated 200 are poisonous and 43 are carcinogenic. These dangerous compounds from second-hand smoke work in a nonsmoker's body the same way that dangerous compounds from mainstream smoke work to damage a smoker's body.

The EPA's report claimed that a fifth of all lung cancers resulted from secondhand smoke. It also estimated that a nonsmoker has a one- or two-in-a-thousand chance of de-

An antismoking billboard in Los Angeles professes the danger of secondhand smoke, a substance not as hazardous as mainstream smoke, but still toxic.

veloping lung cancer because of exposure to secondhand smoke. Because of these risks, the EPA classified second-hand smoke as a Class A carcinogen, a substance as dangerous as benzene (the deadly chemical found in cleaning fluid), asbestos (a natural substance that is closely linked to lung disease), and arsenic (one of the most powerful poisons known). "In other words," stated EPA administrator William K. Reilly, "the risks associated with environmental tobacco smoke are at least an order of magnitude greater than they are for virtually any chemical or risk that EPA regulates." In February 1994 California congressman Henry Waxman, then the chair of the Health and Environment Subcommittee of the House Committee on Energy and Commerce, placed the EPA's figures into perspective. Waxman estimated that more people die each year from inhaling other people's tobacco smoke than die in motor vehicle accidents.

The price of secondhand smoke

In February 1994 a new EPA administrator, Carol Browner, released figures on the financial cost of second-hand smoke. Browner estimated that secondhand smoke costs nonsmokers between $1.5 billion and $3 billion a year, both in medical expenses for treating nonsmokers' illnesses and in the lost earning power resulting from the work nonsmokers missed because of smoking-related illnesses. Browner also calculated the amount of money nonsmokers would have earned had they not died from smoking-related diseases. According to her findings, the American economy loses between $22 billion and $43 billion a year due to the deaths of nonsmokers from secondhand smoke.

A study that appeared in the August 1994 issue of the *Journal of the American College of Cardiology* added to the concern about secondhand smoke. The report claimed that secondhand smoke had resulted in 62,000 fatal heart attacks and 200,000 nonfatal heart attacks in 1985. The study predicted that fewer people would suffer heart attacks from secondhand smoke in 1994, because the

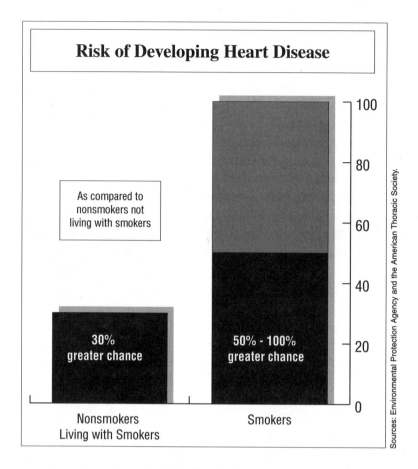

Risk of Developing Heart Disease

As compared to nonsmokers not living with smokers

30% greater chance

50% - 100% greater chance

Nonsmokers Living with Smokers

Smokers

Sources: Environmental Protection Agency and the American Thoracic Society.

number of smokers had declined since 1985. Nevertheless, 47,000 people would die from heart attacks and 150,000 would have nonfatal heart attacks because of secondhand smoke that year. "Heart disease appears to be by far the major mortality risk from passive smoking," the study noted. "Practicing physicians would do well to warn their at-risk heart patients to avoid smoky rooms."

Secondhand smoke and children

Secondhand smoke is particularly harmful to children because often they lack the opportunities to escape from cigarette smoke that nonsmoking adults have. For example, if a child is exposed to cigarette smoke at home, there is very little he or she can do about it. In January 1994 Surgeon General Joycelyn Elders and other government officials estimated that half of all American children live in a home with at least one smoker. Nine million children breathe secondhand smoke regularly.

The EPA has found that a child who lives in a home in which a mother or father smokes runs a much greater chance of developing lower respiratory tract infections than a child who lives in a nonsmoking household. The Environmental Protection Agency has estimated that secondhand smoke—which lowers the resistance of very young children—causes 150,000 to 300,000 such infections each year among children under eighteen months.

The effect on children with asthma, a disease that causes great difficulty in breathing, is even worse. The EPA calculates that secondhand smoke worsens the asthma of 200,000 to 1 million children each year. "Hundreds of thousands of children every year will suffer acute attacks of asthma . . . brought on by secondhand smoke," says Dr. David R. Nielson of Phoenix, a prominent member of the

An estimated 9 million children, such as this one pictured, breathe secondhand smoke on a regular basis. The exposure causes increased chances of respiratory infections and asthma attacks.

American Academy of Otolaryngology (the branch of medicine dealing with the ear, nose, and throat).

Newborn children face especially grave dangers from secondhand smoke, according to a report published in the March 1995 issue of the *Journal of the American Medical Association*. Researchers at the University of California at San Diego studied families in which a child had died from sudden infant death syndrome (SIDS). Every year SIDS causes one out of seven infant deaths in the United States, nearly six thousand fatalities in all. In the Western world SIDS is the leading cause of death among children between the ages of one month and one year. In SIDS deaths, an apparently healthy child's heart simply stops beating. No one is quite sure why. It may have to do with particularly severe reactions to colds or to extreme allergic reactions. It may even have something to do with how a baby lies when it sleeps. The UCSD researchers wondered if these heart failures might be related to smoking, just as other heart disease is.

The UCSD study compared two hundred Southern California infants who had died of SIDS between January 1989 and December 1992 with two hundred healthy infants. The study found that an infant was 3.46 times more likely to die of SIDS if his or her father smoked. If his or her mother smoked, an infant was 2.28 times more likely to die of SIDS. The infant was 2.18 times more likely to fall victim if another adult living in the household smoked. If more than one adult in the household smoked the infant's risk increased by 3.5 times. "It's not enough for a woman to stop smoking while she's pregnant," commented Kenneth C. Schoendorf, a SIDS researcher associated with the National Center for Health Statistics. "It's also important that other people not smoke around the infant."

Efforts to control secondhand smoke

As reports about secondhand smoke began to surface, many nonsmokers became alarmed about their own vulnerability. If smokers wanted to damage their own health, many nonsmokers reasoned, that was their business. But if

"I'VE SMOKED ALL MY LIFE, AND IT NEVER HURT ME!"

their smoke was endangering others—especially children and infants—that was a different matter. To help protect themselves and their children from potentially dangerous smoke, an unprecedented number of nonsmokers joined with the antismoking advocates in calling for government regulation of smoking in public spaces.

The first move to control secondhand smoke occurred in 1969. Based on a study concerning secondhand smoke that it had funded and published, a pioneer antismoking organization known as Action on Smoking and Health (ASH) filed a petition with the Civilian Aviation Board (CAB), a federal agency that regulates air travel. The petition asked that separate smoking and nonsmoking sections be created on passenger aircraft. CAB agreed with ASH and instituted such a program; United Air Lines became the first carrier to implement it. By 1973 separate smoking and nonsmoking sections were mandatory on all U.S. airlines.

In 1971 the federal Department of Health, Education, and Welfare (HEW) followed CAB's lead. HEW secretary Elliot Richardson imposed a series of smoking restrictions in federal buildings, the one area over which HEW had jurisdiction. The next year, the U.S. Interstate Commerce Commission (ICC) placed restrictions on smoking aboard buses that crossed state lines and were thus subject to federal regulation.

Various state legislatures and city councils also began banning smoking in such enclosed places as buses, elevators, and stores, where a nonsmoker not only would have to inhale secondhand smoke directly but also would be forced to inhale that smoke again as the air was recycled by ventilation systems. By 1970 fourteen states had such laws.

Increasing restriction

The first antismoking statutes were fairly limited in scope. In 1972 Betty Carnes, a trustee of Action on Smoking and Health, helped push Arizona into becoming the first state to pass a comprehensive law protecting nonsmokers. The Arizona law prohibited smoking in certain public places, but its basic premise was that smoking was permitted except where it was expressly prohibited. The first state to invert that premise was Minnesota. In 1975 Minnesota's Clean Indoor Air Act banned lighting up in such places as restaurants, private workplaces, and many other public places. And, significantly, smoking was prohibited *except in* specific, well-ventilated areas known as designated smoking areas. The Clean Indoor Air Act was a major victory for antismoking advocates. For the first time, nonsmokers' rights were placed ahead of the rights of smokers.

As evidence of the dangers of secondhand smoke mounted, antismoking laws became tougher and tougher. In 1987 Massachusetts prohibited recently hired police and firefighters from smoking—even *off* the job. Numerous states passed laws restricting public indoor smoking. In 1993 Vermont became the first state to ban *all* indoor smoking. Because of the special dangers secondhand smoke poses to children, the 1994 federal Pro-Children Act banned smoking in public day care centers, schools, Head Start facilities, and other federally funded programs that served children's needs.

Some cities have acted on their own. In 1987 Beverly Hills, California, and Aspen, Colorado, prohibited smoking in all restaurants. In 1993 Los Angeles followed suit. In December 1994 New York City passed legislation outlawing smoking in all public places, including offices, bowling alleys, bingo parlors, restaurants with more than thirty-five seats, outdoor facilities such as Yankee and Shea Stadiums, and the Bronx Zoo. "What the [city]

Mandates to protect nonsmokers from secondhand smoke began in the early 1970s, with separate sections on airplanes for smokers. As laws became tougher, smoking was banned in more public areas.

council is saying, is that you have the right to smoke," remarked New York City Council president Peter F. Vallone, "but you do not have the right to make anyone breathe that smoke. This is a health choice, not a civic choice."

Some observers predicted huge financial losses for such New York City businesses as restaurants and theaters, claiming that smokers would rather stay home and indulge their habit than attend concerts, plays, and restaurants without smoking. "Now people will eat out less often and it is bound to spell economic disaster," said Tom Humber of the National Smokers Alliance. Although some businesses reported a decline in business after the law was enacted, the widespread economic disaster that some predicted did not strike the city. When the antismoking legislation was first proposed, Philip Morris Companies, which is headquartered in Manhattan, threatened to leave New York. Later the tobacco company withdrew the threat.

Even the military has acted to restrict smoking. In January 1994 the navy announced regulations protecting its personnel from secondhand smoke. Smoking would no longer be allowed in the work or living areas of surface ships, although it would still be permitted on open deck areas away from air intake ducts. Sailors on submarines could smoke only in designated areas where the air would be "scrubbed" before being recirculated. Onshore smoking would still be permitted in living quarters but was otherwise seriously restricted. In this way the navy hopes to become "smoke free" by the year 2000, an ambitious goal since 37 percent of naval personnel still smoke, as compared to 20 percent of the U.S. adult population overall.

Private bans on smoking

Federal, state, and local governments have not been the only entities to restrict smoking. Numerous private businesses have also begun to limit smoking inside their establishments. In 1994 the McDonald's fast-food chain banned smoking in fourteen hundred of its company-owned restaurants. Other fast-food chains, including Arby's, Taco Bell, Chuck E. Cheese's, and Dairy Queen, soon followed

suit. In 1995 Dunkin' Donuts went even further, banning smoking in all of its stores, including licensed franchises. By the end of 1994 a third of the enclosed shopping malls in the United States had prohibited smoking. In 1994 Amtrak announced that over 80 percent of its trains would be smoke-free.

A McDonald's Corporation franchise owner displays the no smoking sign. The chain's company-owned as well as many of its franchised restaurants are now completely smoke-free.

Twenty Major League Baseball stadiums have been declared smoke-free, including Cleveland's Jacobs Field and Baltimore's Camden Yards. "We think the restriction of smoking is something that all our fans can live with," said Baltimore Orioles president Larry Lucchino. Some smokers disagree. They feel that imposing smoking restrictions on a largely outdoor venue is ridiculous. "I don't know where you can smoke if not at a ballpark, where the smoke dissipates," said one fan at Camden Yards. This fan

Demonstrators protest a smoking ban in 1988 on domestic flights of less than two hours. As restrictions on smoking become tighter, some smokers feel that their rights are being violated.

is not alone. Many of the 43 million smokers in the United States believe that the efforts to restrict smoking have gone too far, and they want to do something about it.

Smokers' rights

Smoking has been legal in every state of the United States since 1930, when the last prohibitions against smoking were repealed. Smoking is not intoxicating; it does not make smokers reckless or dangerous to others. The risks of smoking are well known. If someone chooses to smoke despite those risks, many insist that is his or her right, just as it is the right of a driver to operate an automobile even though it is well known that automobile accidents kill hundreds of thousands of people each year. As long as smoking is legal, smokers contend, then those who choose to engage in the practice should not be punished.

Many smokers believe their right to equal protection has been eroded by antismoking taxes and bans against smoking in certain areas. They resent being forced out of offices and restaurants and public buildings when they indulge in their legal habit. They object to going without smoking for hours on long plane rides. Increasingly, they feel like second-class citizens. Some have turned to the courts for relief.

"Banished to the garage"

One example is Diane Bacon, a secretary for a law firm in Chevy Chase, Maryland. When her firm moved to a new building, the owners of the firm decided to restrict smoking to private offices. That was fine for smokers who *had* private offices, but it rankled smokers who worked in open areas—mainly lower-level clerical workers. Bacon was among those who were upset. "I told them, 'If you need me, you can just look out the window and holler.'"

Some of the firm's lawyers took up Bacon's cause and that of others like her. Attorney Marianne Loman, who had smoked for thirty years, successfully fought for an inside smoking area for those clerical staff who did not have private offices and who therefore could not legally smoke indoors. "I was rather vehement," Loman told the *Washington Post*, "that there be [a place for secretaries to smoke] so they wouldn't be banished to the garage. I won that one."

Loman is one of millions of smokers who resent the fact that nonsmokers are increasingly restricting their right to smoke and are increasingly assertive about lecturing smokers on the dangers of smoking. "I find it rude that perfect strangers talk to me like I'm some kind of idiot," Loman continues. "I wouldn't go up to somebody who's overweight and eating beef and say, 'You shouldn't be doing that.'" According to Loman, reformed smokers are the worst. "They're the most self-righteous," she complains.

Many smokers share Loman's resentment toward nonsmokers, but some do not. Outside a new smoke-free office building in West Los Angeles, smokers not only have to go outdoors but have to smoke behind the building near a garbage dumpster. One of those smokers, Susan Castor, a production assistant for a cable TV company, is sympathetic to the wishes of nonsmokers. "I'd just as soon smoke out here and not have my smoke bother anyone," Castor says. "I think it should be that way."

Not surprisingly, the tobacco industry is quick to offer support to customers like Loman. Paid spokespersons lobby long and hard against each new antismoking warning, restriction, and ban that is proposed. They claim that restrictions on smoking constitute "social engineering on a vast scale . . . recalling the extremism of Prohibition," referring not to the earlier bans on smoking but to the constitutional prohibition of the manufacture, transportation, and sale of alcohol ratified in 1919.

The prohibition of alcohol proved unworkable and divisive and was repealed within a few years, and many smokers and pro-smoking lobbyists worry that antismoking

"THEY DON'T LOOK LIKE PASSIVE SMOKERS TO ME...."

activists are driving the nation toward a similar crisis. Outlawing tobacco, they argue, will create a vast illegal market for the popular product, just as the ban on alcohol did in the 1920s and the ban on illegal drugs does today. Such action will add to the already severe crime problem in America: Gangs will fight to control the illegal trade, and millions of otherwise law-abiding citizens will become criminals for indulging in a habit they practiced legally for years. At the same time, the government will lose the money it derives from taxing legal tobacco products.

California congressman Henry Waxman contends that comparing antismoking measures to Prohibition is unfair and inaccurate. "The right analogy," Waxman claims, "is drunk driving. Our laws [today] don't ban drinking, but they do ban drinking while you drive because of the risk to others." John Banzhof, the executive director of the antismoking group Action on Smoking and Health, agrees that the risk to others is at the heart of the antismoking debate. "Anyone who lights up in public places can't really say they are being considerate of others," he says. "It's like spraying asbestos fibers in the air and saying you're being considerate to others if you're not spraying it directly in their faces."

Statistics and skeptics

Are the dangers of secondhand smoke really comparable to those posed by asbestos fibers and other proven killers? Some scientists doubt it. They point out that research on secondhand smoke is relatively new, that its results are tentative, that not all studies on the subject conclude that secondhand smoke is dangerous, and that those that do may be flawed. For example, an agency within the federal government questions the results of the EPA's influential 1994 report about the effects of secondhand smoke. Members of the Congressional Research Service (CRS), an arm of the Library of Congress, question the EPA's statistical analysis and its methods of assessing data from other studies. "Our evaluation," says Jane G. Gravelle, a senior specialist in economic policy for the

A man smokes while attending a smokers' rights meeting conducted by a tobacco company representative. The tobacco industry supports pro-smoking lobbyists and encourages smokers to stand up for their rights.

CRS, "was that the statistical analysis does not appear to support a conclusion that there [were] substantial health effects of passive smoking." Reworking the EPA's statistics, the CRS estimated nonsmoker lung cancer deaths from secondhand smoke to be six hundred annually—one-fifth the EPA's estimate of three thousand.

The CRS is not alone in its skepticism. Not all of the studies that the EPA used to reach its conclusions on the dangers of secondhand smoke point conclusively to that same finding. And not every study on secondhand smoke was consulted by the EPA. For example, the EPA failed to include a study of 618 Missouri women who were either former smokers or lifetime nonsmokers. That study (funded by the National Cancer Institute) found no risk of increased lung cancer for nonsmokers inhaling second-hand smoke during childhood or in the workplace or from living with a spouse who smoked up to a pack of ciga-rettes a day for less than forty years.

Such data cause many to question whether secondhand smoke is the culprit the EPA says it is. "I think we are jus-tified in approaching the EPA report with considerable skepticism," comments Charlie Rose, a former North Car-olina congressman who represented tobacco interests in his home state. "This is not the first time that questions have been raised about the agency's scientific competence."

The confidence interval

The EPA's critics also point out that the agency reached its conclusions using a lower so-called confidence interval than normal. A confidence interval is a tool statisticians use to compensate for undetectable errors in a given study. Most researchers use a confidence interval of 95 percent (meaning they state their conclusions with 95 percent cer-tainty, or confidence), but the EPA used a confidence in-terval of only 90 percent. "Although this may seem like a marginal difference," charges Matthew C. Hoffman, an an-alyst with the Competitive Enterprise Institute, "it is actu-ally a major leap; it doubles the probability that the result of the study is due to chance."

John Shanahan of the Heritage Foundation also criticizes the EPA's decision to lower the confidence interval. "While lower confidence levels theoretically can be used, answers derived from them are much less reliable," writes Shanahan. "Consequently, scientists don't tend to use them."

Stanton Glantz, a scientist at the EPA, defends the use of the 90 percent confidence interval. "There is nothing magical about [the 95 percent level]," says Glantz. "I know that scientifically it's widely used, but there is a

strong body of thought that people are too slavishly tied to 95 percent." Other EPA officials note that the independent panel that reviewed the study found no problem with the 90 percent confidence interval. "We had a clear consensus," comments Morton Lippman, who headed the review committee. "The EPA reached the right conclusion."

The battle over secondhand smoke is central to the war over smokers' rights. If secondhand smoke is harmless, or its dangers are greatly exaggerated, smokers and the tobacco companies will no doubt lobby to have antismoking laws repealed. If the EPA's findings are confirmed, then federal, state, and local governments will continue to wrestle with the problem of where to allow public smoking, if they allow it at all.

5

Teens and Smoking

MOST SMOKERS ARE adults, but relatively few people *start* smoking as adults. Despite all the laws against underage smoking (every state and the District of Columbia ban cigarette sales to people under eighteen) and all the warnings to teens from health agencies, teachers, and parents, the vast majority of smokers first experiment with tobacco as teenagers.

Each day four thousand American minors begin smoking. Researchers say that the average teen smoker begins experimenting with cigarettes at age thirteen. By the middle of the fourteenth year, it is a daily habit. "Eighty percent of all adult smokers light up that first cigarette before their eighteenth birthday," says Health and Human Services secretary Donna Shalala. "We're not talking about an innocent habit. We are talking about a pediatric disease that must be stopped."

Recent increase in teen smoking—especially in young teens

Until recently it seemed that health officials were making progress in this regard. For decades, the number of new teenage smokers declined steadily. In the 1990s, though, the trend reversed itself. From 1991 through 1995 the percentage of high school students who had smoked within the previous month rose from 27.5 percent to 34.8 percent. Among eighth-grade students the situation was worse; the number of eighth-grade smokers grew by a full one-third. A 1995 study by University of Michigan

Smooth marketing.

KIRK ©91

researchers reported that tobacco use by teens had increased to its highest level since 1979.

Why teens smoke

Most young people start smoking for one of two basic reasons: to conform to the behavior of the people around them, or to rebel against it. Most teenage smokers start smoking to conform; they want to emulate the behavior of their parents, teachers, or friends who smoke. Smoking may make them feel more adult, more like the people they admire. Statistics show that if a parent smokes, there is a greater chance his or her children will smoke. "The more the parents smoke," says Scott Ward of the University of Pennsylvania, "the more likely the child will smoke; the more the parents discourage smoking the less likely the child will smoke."

On the other hand, most teenagers at some point have a strong need to express their independence from their parents. Instead of copying what their parents do, they often rebel against it. A child of nonsmoking parents may take up the habit to demonstrate his or her independence from their wishes and beliefs. Of course, this tendency can work to discourage smoking: The children of smokers, for example, are as likely to oppose the habit.

Paradoxically, teens may start smoking to simultaneously rebel and conform. They may wish to rebel against their parents or authority in general and at the same time feel a need to conform to the behavior of their peers. They smoke because their friends smoke and because it makes them feel cool, different from their parents. Studies show that more than half of teen smokers say they took their first puff with a friend.

The youth market

Tobacco companies are aware of the many—and sometimes contradictory—reasons why teenagers smoke. Knowing that the vast majority of smokers begin as teenagers, tobacco company executives must ensure that the public image of smoking is in sync with the wants and needs of American youth. By law, the tobacco companies cannot promote their products directly to underage smokers, and most companies do not. Yet they cannot afford to ignore the market, either. To capture the business of legal customers on the day they turn eighteen, a tobacco company needs to appeal to them when they are seventeen, sixteen, or younger.

Tobacco companies promote their public image in many ways. For example, they might pay a motion picture company to use their products in a movie, an arrangement known as a product placement. The association of a product with a certain character or movie can boost sales for the company that obtains the product placement. Until 1990 the tobacco industry routinely paid for product placements to get cigarettes into films. Since 1990, however, that practice seems to have declined.

Many observers believe tobacco companies have stopped paying for product placements because smoking is already prominent in many movies. Like the stars of the 1930s and 1940s, the most appealing characters in today's movies often are shown smoking. Sharon Stone in *Basic Instinct*, Uma Thurman in *Pulp Fiction* and *The Truth About Cats and Dogs*, and Winona Ryder in *How to Make an American Quilt* are just a few of the glamorous actresses seductively dragging on cigarettes in recent films. "I think if a Martian went to the movies today," remarks Professor Stanton A. Glantz, "it would think most people here smoke and those who do are the most desirable people."

Some critics claim it's no coincidence that teen smoking has dramatically increased at the same time smoking on the silver screen has similarly skyrocketed. "There's a hell of a lot of smoking in movies these days," notes syndicated columnist Jeff Greenfield, "and there seems to be an in-

A young boy lights one cigarette from another. After a decrease in youth smoking that spanned decades, the 1990s have seen a sharp reversal of the trend.

crease in teenage smoking. Hollywood is a community that wears its heart on its sleeve, but what about our lungs?"

Movie and television stars are not the only celebrities who can influence the behavior of the public. Professional athletes also can shape the behavior of their fans. For this reason, athletes are paid enormous sums of money to endorse products. Tobacco companies are not allowed to air commercials on television and radio, but they are able to associate their products with athletes by sponsoring televised sporting events such as automobile races, motorcycle races, and tennis tournaments. At these events large billboards featuring cigarette brands are placed within camera range, broadcast again and again to viewers at home. During one ninety-minute telecast of an auto race, the name Marlboro appeared on television 5,993 times.

The makers of smokeless tobacco products often sponsor events, as well. Skoal and Copenhagen are two

A teenage girl exhales as she lights a cigarette for her friend. Some people claim that there is a relationship between the prevalence of smoking in movies and the rise in teen smoking.

companies that feature their products at professional rodeos, "monster" truck racing, drag racing, sprint racing, and stock car racing. The result is the same as cigarette sponsorship: heavy TV visibility and an increase in sales.

Cigarette advertising

The most direct and powerful way to shape a public image is through advertising. The tobacco industry has been one of the largest advertisers in history. Even since tobacco companies were barred from producing television and radio commercials, their advertising spending has gone up. In 1981 the industry's advertising and promotion budget amounted to $1.5 billion. By 1988 it had grown to $3.3 billion. In just five years that figure has skyrocketed to $5.23 billion.

Critics of the tobacco industry have charged that cigarette companies target their ads to appeal to young people. These critics point out that with the exception of the famous "Marlboro Man," very few ads feature older people. Most cigarette advertising features youthful, vibrant, exciting, sophisticated people smoking. This approach appeals to younger people who feel that they too can be as glamorous as the people they see in cigarette ads. "The models are always young, good-looking, and popular," says preteen Daniel Candelaria. "People who buy the cigarettes think if they can smoke and be pretty and thin and have fun, maybe I can too." Another preteen, Tana Swink, explains why it would pay for a tobacco company to attract an underage smoker to its brand. "If the cigarette companies can get kids hooked on a brand," says Swink, "then they just might buy that brand their whole life."

Tobacco executives deny that their advertising program is aimed at young people, or even at adult nonsmokers. They claim that their ads are designed merely to get those who already smoke to change from one brand to another. Critics of the tobacco industry question the economics of this claim. They point out that only 10 percent of smokers switch brands each year. If the tobacco companies spend more than $5 billion a year on advertising and promotion, then they are spending $345 a year in advertising for every smoker who switches brands. Considering that the average smoker spends only $347 a year on cigarettes, critics contend that the industry's efforts hardly make sense economically. "The industry knows [the brand-switching argument is] nonsense," says former advertising executive Emerson Foote. "I am always amused by the suggestion that advertising, a function that has been shown to increase consumption of every other product, somehow fails to work with tobacco products."

Cigarette manufacturers are criticized for targeting adolescents with ads like these, showing young, beautiful people having fun.

The tobacco companies disagree. They point out that smokers can remain loyal to one brand for many years, so the cost of getting them to switch can be justified over time. Besides, they say, if they did not advertise, they would be unable to replace the customers who do switch brands, sales would fall, and they would be forced out of business.

Joe Camel

Other critics insist that the economics of advertising proves that the tobacco companies advertise to attract new smokers rather than convince existing ones to switch brands. These critics are disturbed by the content of the ads, especially those that use cartoon characters, which they claim is blatantly designed to appeal to underage, beginning smokers.

The most famous example of a successful cartoon advertising campaign for a cigarette company is that conducted by R. J. Reynolds, makers of Camel cigarettes. In 1988 the company unveiled a new advertising campaign built around a cartoon camel called Old Joe Camel. Joe Camel epitomized coolness and hipness, and he appeared almost everywhere—in ads, on billboards, in stores, on the sides of passing buses. Illustrated with rich colors and unusual perspectives, Joe Camel grabbed the attention of young and old alike. Before long children as young as age three were able to recognize Joe Camel, and thus identify with the Camel brand and the entire concept of smoking. Ninety-one percent of six-year-olds could recognize Joe Camel. Some surveys even contended he was more famous than Mickey Mouse.

As Camel's recognition by youngsters skyrocketed, so did its sales to underage smokers. Between 1988 and 1990 teenage smokers who smoked Camels increased sixty-six-fold, from just 0.5 percent to 33 percent. Camel sales to those between the ages of twelve and nineteen increased from just $6 million in 1988 to $476 million in 1991.

Many people feel these sales figures are neither accidental nor coincidental, that the Joe Camel ad campaign

was clearly aimed at enticing youngsters to smoke. "Let's end the hypocrisy of pretending that while sales to teens are illegal, marketing to teens is legal," said President Bill Clinton in August 1995. "Let's stop pretending that a cartoon character in a funny costume is trying to sell to adults, not children."

Banning Joe Camel violates rights

R. J. Reynolds vigorously denies Joe Camel is aimed at young people. "We have never seen any evidence that the Joe Camel character has caused kids to want to start smoking," says company spokesperson Peggy Carter, who points out that Marlboro is the brand actually favored by underage smokers. "It has all been conjecture."

Among those defending the Camel brand's right to use the Joe Camel character is the American Civil Liberties Union (ACLU), known for its vigorous defense of

Opponents of the Joe Camel ad campaign claim that the cartoon character is specifically geared toward children. In the first two years of the campaign, the sale of Camels to teens rose nearly 33 percent.

A teenager smokes outside his school. Although many people are concerned about teen smoking and would like to ban the Joe Camel ads, others say that this type of censorship is unconstitutional.

individual rights. When tobacco companies went to court to block controls on tobacco advertising, the ACLU argued that R. J. Reynolds's constitutional rights would be violated if Joe Camel was banned. They warned that such a ban would set a dangerous precedent, making it easier to censor other forms of advertising and speech. They worried that if the government could tell tobacco companies what images they should use in paid advertising, it might begin to dictate what images other types of companies could use, then attempt to control other forms of speech.

False advertising

Antismoking advocates point out, however, that the ACLU might not have been arguing the issue on purely constitutional grounds. Within a five-year period the organization has accepted $5 million in contributions from the tobacco industry. Besides, antismoking activists point out, the government routinely restricts, regulates, and punishes speech that poses special dangers to society. False and deceptive advertising is one of several forms of speech the

U.S. Supreme Court has declared to be outside the protection of the First Amendment to the Constitution, which states that "Congress shall make no law abridging . . . freedom of speech, or of the press." Cigarette advertising that portrays smoking as a healthy or innocuous habit—especially for young people—might be deemed false and/or deceptive, and thus be subject to a government ban.

The Supreme Court also has ruled that the government can restrict speech that incites lawless behavior. Since it is illegal for minors to smoke, advertising that encourages them to take up the habit could meet the high court's test for incitement. "The question in every case," wrote Justice Oliver Wendell Holmes Jr. in the first legal definition of incitement, "is whether the words are used in such circumstances and are of such a nature as to create a clear and present danger that they will bring about the substantive evils that Congress has the right to prevent." Ads depicting

Demonstrators march in front of a large tobacco company's headquarters, demanding that it stop marketing cigarettes to children.

Joe Camel, antismoking advocates argue, clearly meet this legal test.

In 1991 the Coalition on Smoking and Health urged the Federal Trade Commission (FTC) to ban Joe Camel ads, charging they were aimed directly at children. At one point the entire staff of the FTC wrote a letter to R. J. Reynolds, demanding the ads be banned. So did more than half the nation's state attorneys general. Only with the proposal of federal regulations in 1996 is the industry expected to remove cartoon characters from tobacco products.

Secret marketing plans

Although the tobacco industry publicly asserts that it wants teens to wait until they are adults before they make the decision whether or not to take up the tobacco habit, internal tobacco company memos suggest otherwise. In 1988 Canada passed a law controlling the marketing of tobacco. Two Canadian tobacco companies connected to American tobacco companies sued to overturn its provisions. In the process, however, many of their internal documents revealed their interests in reaching the teenage market.

Marketing plans revealed that some "target groups" started at age twelve. "Young smokers," one document reads, "represent the major opportunity group for the cigarette industry. We should therefore determine their attitude to smoking and health and how this might change over time." The plans also said that company ads should portray activities that would appeal to teenagers—vigorous, athletic, glamorous activities. "The activity shown," indicates one 1981 memo, "should be one which is practiced by young people sixteen to twenty years old, or one that these people can reasonably aspire to in the near future."

The tobacco company's studies even deal with kids who want to quit smoking. Since youngsters are starting to smoke at earlier ages, they often want to quit at earlier ages. Someone who had started smoking at, say, age twelve might want to quit at age sixteen or seventeen. "The desire to quit seems to come earlier now than before,

Although cigarette sales are prohibited to people under eighteen, vending machines, such as this one, are seldom monitored and are an easy way for children to obtain cigarettes.

even prior to the end of high school," one in-depth industry study of the teen market revealed. "However, the desire to quit and actually carrying it out, are two quite different things, as the would-be quitter soon learns."

Vending machines

All fifty states bar cigarette sales to minors, but antismoking laws leave plenty of loopholes through which a teenager can grab a pack of cigarettes. For example, cigarette vending machines are easy for teenagers to find and use. Since they are unattended, teenagers can avoid having to face a store clerk and produce proof of age to obtain cigarettes.

Laws prohibit those under eighteen from obtaining a wide variety of items besides tobacco. They cannot buy beer, wine, or hard liquor. They cannot buy adult magazines or firearms. However, none of these other items are available to *anyone* from vending machines where little control exists over who can purchase a product. It is hard to imagine buying a can of Budweiser or a box of shotgun shells from a vending machine, but anyone, including minors, can easily purchase cigarettes from one. "For cigarettes, you just go anywhere," says fourteen-year-old Robert Caldwell. "Put twelve quarters into one of those machines, take it, and go."

In 1992 New York State, aiming to decrease the number and location of cigarette vending machines, limited their use to bars, private clubs, and private businesses with little public contact. The law has so far failed to prevent New York's teen smoking rate from inching upward (part of a national trend) since the law was passed.

But even in Virginia, a tobacco-growing state with generally pro-smoking governmental policies, legislation has tightened teen access to cigarette vending machines. In February 1996 the state legislature passed a bill mandating that machines be within a clerk's eyesight or ten feet from a public entrance. It is too early to know how effective this new statute will be.

The FDA takes action

Because of the continuing existence, and growth, of teen smoking, in August 1995 the Food and Drug Administration announced a wide-ranging set of proposals designed to deal with the problem. The overall effect of the FDA program would be to limit teen access to cigarettes and to restrict tobacco industry efforts to reach the youth market.

A key FDA proposal would mandate a federal minimum purchase age of eighteen. The agency also wished to ban cigarette vending machines, the giving away of free samples of cigarettes, mail-order sales of cigarettes, and self-service cigarette displays. The FDA also wanted all cigarette retailers to verify that their customers were actually eighteen before selling them cigarettes.

Furthermore, the Food and Drug Administration wanted to severely limit the type of advertising or promotion that tobacco critics claimed was aimed at young people. The FDA proposal contained three key elements regarding advertising and promotion:

• Pictures and illustrations would be banned from cigarette ads and labels. In the future, these ads and labels could only have text. This would mean the end of such controversial ad campaigns as the one featuring cartoon character Joe Camel.

• The sale or distribution of such merchandise as caps or T-shirts that feature cigarette brand logos would also be prohibited.

• Tobacco companies would no longer be allowed to sponsor athletic events, concerts, and exhibitions that

Advertising cigarettes on clothing, like this Joe Camel jacket, would no longer be allowed under proposed FDA restrictions, which also include banning pictures from ads altogether.

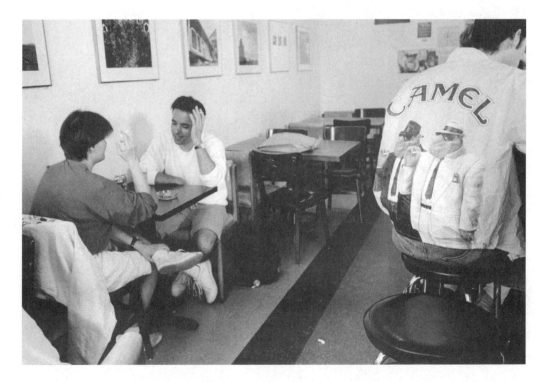

featured the brand name of the cigarette in the title of the event. These events, however, could continue to be named for the corporation itself.

The FDA's proposed regulations would also require tobacco companies to create and maintain a nationwide campaign aimed at discouraging adolescents and children from smoking.

The tobacco industry responded by suing the Food and Drug Administration, claiming it had no jurisdiction over cigarettes because they are not a drug and because Congress has not specifically granted authority over cigarettes to the FDA. The FDA, the industry claimed, was overreaching its authority.

"Plaintiff tobacco companies do not make any claims of therapeutic purpose for their cigarettes [that is, that cigarettes are drugs]," their complaint read. "Their cigarettes are promoted solely for smoking pleasure." Tobacco-industry

Two teenage girls hang out and smoke with some friends. The FDA wants the tobacco industry to stop marketing to minors and to implement a campaign to discourage teens from smoking.

lawyers supported their case with five hundred pages of documentation.

In August 1996, however, President Bill Clinton announced that much of the FDA's program would be implemented by the federal government.

"Today I know better"

If the tobacco companies cannot be convinced to leave teenagers and preteens alone until they are adults, then public officials will feel pressure to take more drastic steps to protect today's youth.

Because of the continued resistance to any form of regulation, many of these officials question the sincerity of the tobacco industry to voluntarily police itself regarding sales to teenagers. Among those people is former president Jimmy Carter. "During my administration," Carter wrote in an August 1995 *USA Today* editorial, "the industry used its power and persuasion to argue, just as it is doing today, that it could be trusted not to market cigarettes to children. Like many public officials at that time, I believed the industry could be persuaded to behave responsibly. . . . Today I know better."

6

Making the Tobacco Companies Pay

MANY PEOPLE WHO are opposed to smoking have turned to the U.S. Congress, state legislatures, and local governments for legislative and administrative relief from the dangers posed by smoking. Others have turned to the courts for judgments against the tobacco companies for deceiving the public about many aspects of smoking, including its health risks and its addictive qualities. As a result of this deception, litigants argue, millions of people have suffered from preventable diseases and addictions. They believe the tobacco companies are legally liable as well as morally responsible; and they seek to make them pay for the harm their products cause.

Beginning the court battle

The first lawsuit against a tobacco company by a smoker was filed in 1954. A lung cancer patient sued the Liggett & Myers company, charging it with negligence in marketing a product that had contributed to the plaintiff's contracting cancer. The case, known as *Pritchett v. Liggett & Myers*, dragged on for thirteen years. No longer able to bear the cost of the action, the plaintiff eventually dropped the suit.

Another lung cancer patient took a slightly different approach in another early tobacco company lawsuit. In *Green v. American Tobacco Co.*, the plaintiff charged that cigarettes were a violation of the Pure Food and Drug Act, a federal statute that was designed to protect American consumers from tainted food and dangerous or ineffective drugs. In other words, the plaintiff alleged that the American Tobacco Company was selling an unsafe product. For proof of the harmful effects of cigarettes, the plaintiff offered his own medical history. Green won his initial suit, but the tobacco company appealed the verdict. The appeals court dismissed Green's argument, ruling that any contribution smoking made to lung cancer was "wholly irrelevant" to American Tobacco's legal liability.

Many people would like to see the tobacco industry pay for manufacturing addictive and disease-causing products and deceiving the public about the dangers of smoking.

The trial judge in a later lawsuit disagreed with this appeals court ruling. In *Wilks v. American Tobacco Co.*, a case involving the death of a smoker, the judge instructed the jury that "cigarettes are defective" and that tobacco companies really did have an "absolute liability" in terms of financial payments for the damage cigarettes were alleged to cause. The jury, however, was not convinced that lung cancer caused the plaintiff's death, so it did not award the plaintiff's family any money.

The findings in these cases were typical. Between 1950 and 1990, more than five hundred lawsuits were launched against the tobacco industry. Only eighteen went to trial, and the tobacco industry lost none. No one received a cent in damages.

"Just what the doctor ordered"

A case involving a New Jersey woman, Rose Cipollone, came close to breaking the cigarette companies' judicial winning streak. Mrs. Cipollone began smoking as a sixteen-year-old in 1942. She smoked Chesterfields and L&Ms in part because she believed their manufacturers' advertising claims of product safety and in part because she was influenced by the sophisticated movie stars she saw smoking. Even as a child she thought cigarettes were glamorous. "We used to roll up little pieces of paper," she recalled, "and we used to walk around the house with these high heels and those old-fashioned long dresses and with the cigarettes, and we were playing movie star or grownup."

In 1982, nearly fifteen thousand packs of cigarettes later, Rose Cipollone contracted lung cancer. Surgeons removed one of her lungs, but tobacco's hold over her was so strong that she remained a smoker. "All I know," she admitted, "is that I had to smoke. I would panic if I didn't have cigarettes around me." However, Mrs. Cipollone and her husband, Antonio, decided to sue the Liggett Tobacco Group, which manufactured both of the brands she smoked. Their legal strategy was to prove the company had used misleading advertising. They argued that

This ad claiming L&M Filters to be "Just what the doctor ordered" led Rose Cipollone to believe that smoking this brand of cigarettes would not harm her health.

Liggett's claims that L&Ms were "Just what the doctor ordered" and that a smoker should "Play safe. Smoke Chesterfields" were deliberately misleading. According to Mrs. Cipollone, these ads gave her a false sense of security and persuaded her that smoking these brands would not cause illness.

An important feature of this case was the evidence of thousands of internal documents released by the defendants to the court. This was one of the earliest instances of a tobacco company's making public such internal memos. One 1961 memo was particularly damaging and seemed to reveal that the company knew a great deal about the dangers of its products. It read in part: "There are biologically active materials in cigarette tobacco that are (a) cancer causing (b) cancer promoting (c) poisonous (d) stimulating, pleasurable and flavorful."

In 1984, at age fifty-eight, Rose Cipollone died of lung cancer. Her husband continued the lawsuit. The defendants argued that they were not responsible for Rose

Antonio Cipollone, right, smiles after winning $400,000 in damages from the Liggett Tobacco Group. Liggett appealed the decision and eventually the Cipollone children could no longer bear the cost of the lawsuit.

Cipollone's death, that smoking had not been proved to cause cancer, and that the type of cancer that killed Mrs. Cipollone had not even been statistically linked to cigarettes. They also argued that Rose Cipollone was an independent person, capable of making informed judgments, and that she had chosen to smoke with full knowledge of the risks involved.

On June 13, 1988, a federal district court found in favor of Antonio Cipollone. The court held that Liggett should "have warned consumers [prior to 1966, the date warning labels were first placed on cigarette packs,] regarding the health risks of smoking." It awarded Cipollone $400,000 in damages, the first time monetary damages had been leveled against a tobacco company in such a case. Liggett appealed the judgment. Shortly thereafter, Antonio Cipollone also died, but the Cipollones' children decided to pursue the case.

In 1990 a Philadelphia appeals court threw out the verdict, saying the tobacco companies were protected by a legal doctrine called preemption. The court declared that when Congress forced the tobacco industry to place warning labels on cigarettes in 1966 it freed manufacturers from any blame for the health risks of their product. Consumers had been warned about those risks, the court reasoned: if they continued to smoke, that was their responsibility.

The court did not apply the doctrine of preemption to the period before the warning labels first appeared on cigarette packs, however. Because Mrs. Cipollone had started to smoke in 1942, the Cipollone family and its attorneys believed the doctrine of preemption did not apply to her. They appealed the case to the U.S. Supreme Court. In June 1992 the Court ruled 7-2 in the Cipollones' favor and sent the case back to a state court for retrial.

Tobacco spokespersons said they were not worried about the landmark decision, but most saw it as a major defeat for cigarette companies. "Now that the court has made it possible for people to . . . hold the industry accountable for deceptive practices," said Harvard Law professor Lawrence Tribe, "it will be really quite a new day for these lawsuits."

Attorney Marc Edell had been there from the beginning and was less optimistic than Tribe. "[The tobacco industry's] approach," Edell said, "has always been, 'We'll outlast anybody.' They have very talented spin doctors who will put this in a favorable light. But the case opened up for us broad new vistas of liability."

Just as Edell predicted, the tobacco companies managed to outlast the Cipollone family. The family's legal bills mounted, and in December 1992—nine years after the lawsuit began and six after Rose Cipollone died of lung cancer—the family withdrew the lawsuit. In doing so, they were barred by law from ever reopening the case. The tobacco companies were able to breathe easily again.

State lawsuits

Although few individuals can afford to undertake a court challenge that might last many years, state governments often can. Recently they have. Lawyers for the states maintain that the tobacco companies are liable for the money the states have to spend to care for residents who become sick and die from smoking. More than a dozen states—including Florida, Mississippi, Minnesota, Massachusetts, and West Virginia—have sued tobacco companies to recover public funds spent on those suffering from smoking-related diseases.

The amounts of money involved are staggering. For example, in August 1994, Minnesota attorney general Hu-

This antismoking demonstration illustrates the growing support for making tobacco companies take responsibility for the effects of their products.

bert Humphrey III and Minnesota Blue Cross combined to sue the tobacco industry for $350 million, the sum of forty years of tobacco-related medical costs.

The state decided to file suit after receiving internal tobacco industry documents describing a meeting of tobacco executives in December 1953. In the meeting the participants discussed early reports about tobacco's harmfulness and decided to launch a public relations campaign that promised to keep the public informed about the issue. Instead, the Minnesota suit said, the companies covered up what they found about tobacco's dangers. Instead of reporting any of it, company officials continued to issue statements saying there was no danger in using their products. The plaintiffs also charged that the tobacco companies had violated the state's consumer safety laws by marketing an unsafe product. Humphrey also argued that by cooperating in their promotion of tobacco, the companies had violated antitrust statutes (laws designed to minimize unfair business practices or monopolies). "Previous lawsuits have said the tobacco companies should pay because their products are dangerous," said Humphrey. "This suit says they should pay because their conduct is illegal."

Mississippi sues tobacco companies

As Minnesota's case moved slowly through the courts, other states also launched their own suits against the industry. In December 1994 Mississippi attorney general Mike Moore filed suit against thirteen tobacco companies for selling products he claimed they knew were harmful. This suit went far beyond earlier cases that targeted only cigarette-producing companies. It also went after others who engaged in the sale of cigarettes—distributors, trade organizations, and even a public relations firm that marketed cigarettes.

Moore alleged that the defendants' actions in making, selling, and marketing cigarettes in Mississippi had resulted in Medicaid costs of between $60 and $80 million a year, borne by the state's taxpayers. "This, to me, is the most important health litigation ever filed in America," said

A seventy-nine-year-old victim of severe lung disease attends a rally at the Capitol. The toll cigarettes have taken on the public's health has prompted several states to take legal action against the tobacco industry.

Moore, "so every hearing is going to be vitally important. They have made hundreds of millions of dollars in profit and the taxpayers have stood by and cleaned up the mess."

Billions of dollars in damages

In early 1995 the state of Florida sued to recover the $1.43 billion it said smoking-related illnesses and deaths had cost its taxpayers. Later in 1995, the states of West Virginia and Maryland announced they would also sue tobacco companies to recover Medicaid costs for sick smokers, a threat they have since carried out. Maryland governor Parris Glendening said his state would seek $50 million in damages to pay for treating "people who are made sick by an industry that refuses to take responsibility for its action." Maryland officials estimated that smoking imposed costs of $1.5 billion a year on state residents and that six thousand Marylanders died annually from smoking-related diseases.

As the tobacco companies prepared their defenses against lawsuits filed by state governments, they were hit with another type of legal action, class action suits. In a class action suit, the plaintiffs file suit and seek damages on behalf of everyone in a group that has been harmed in some way. If the plaintiffs win, they must share the proceeds of their suit with anyone who can show he or she belongs in the group of people who were harmed.

The Castano class action suit

In 1994 a class action suit known as *Castano v. American Tobacco* was initiated against the nation's five largest tobacco companies: R. J. Reynolds, American Tobacco, Lorillard Tobacco, Philip Morris, and Liggett & Myers. The plaintiffs—three smokers and the widow of a smoker who died of cancer, Dianne Castano—claimed to speak for all smokers who were addicted to tobacco.

Previous cases against the tobacco industry had centered on the diseases the plaintiffs said smoking had caused. They had often failed because tobacco companies had successfully argued that smokers had been warned and were free to choose whether to smoke or not. This case was different. The plaintiffs claimed that there was no free choice for smokers, that because of the nicotine cigarettes contained smokers were addicted to a disease-causing substance and could not easily stop.

In earlier cases against the tobacco industry, plaintiffs were often worn down by the cost of litigation as they battled an industry with over $40 billion in annual domestic revenue. The odds were slightly better in the Castano case, whose plaintiffs had at their disposal 120 lawyers nationwide from sixty different law firms, including some of the nation's most experienced and skillful class action lawyers. These law firms were so serious about winning this case that when they first met to decide strategy, each brought with them a $25,000 check to help fund their cause.

The Castano case is significant because it is the first tobacco class action case to be allowed into a federal court. The federal jurisdiction increased the scope of the class action to include smokers across the United States, and the total amount of damages sought reached the $100 million mark.

The plaintiffs charged the defendants, along with the Tobacco Institute, a public relations and research arm of the tobacco industry, with concealing research that nicotine was addictive. They also alleged that the companies had manipulated levels of nicotine found in cigarettes to keep smokers addicted. "What we are going to show," said one attorney, "is that the freedom of choice was taken away. [Tobacco companies] knew and calculated [cigarettes] would addict, and they never warned against it."

In March 1996, Liggett & Myers, manufacturer of such cigarette brands as L&M, Chesterfield, Lark, Eve, and the discount brand Pyramid, broke ranks with the other defendants and settled out of court. While not admitting guilt,

Mike Smith for the *Las Vegas Sun*. Reprinted with permission.

Liggett & Myers, the smallest of the five firms named in the suit, agreed that for the next twenty-five years it would pay up to 12 percent of its pretax income, $2 million a year or a total of $50 million, to fund smoking cessation programs and to study nicotine addiction.

Liggett & Myers also agreed to drop out of a lawsuit that tobacco companies had brought to block proposals the Food and Drug Administration first made in August 1995 to curb underage smoking. These proposals would limit such things as color in tobacco advertisements, brand-name cigarette ads on such merchandise as caps and T-shirts, and tobacco sponsorship of sporting events such as tennis tournaments and auto races. It would also limit tobacco advertising in publications that have a large underage readership. Furthermore, Liggett & Myers announced that it would abide by some of the FDA proposals designed to prevent teen smoking. For example, the company agreed to no longer use cartoon characters to advertise cigarettes and to limit the free distribution of cigarettes. Some observers claimed that these nonmonetary concessions were far more significant than the cash payments the company promised to make.

Medical compensation

Liggett & Myers further announced it would settle the lawsuits brought by the attorneys general of Florida, Massachusetts, Minnesota, Mississippi, and West Virginia. The tobacco giant agreed to pay the states $135 million to compensate for past and present medical costs. If other states participated in this settlement, Liggett & Myers would also contribute between 2 and 7 percent of its pretax income over a twenty-five-year period to various programs designed to help smokers kick the habit. On the same day Liggett & Myers announced the settlement, the state of Louisiana brought suit against the tobacco industry to recoup the health care costs of its smokers.

Most of the states involved accepted the settlement. "We hope this will be a trail-blazing agreement that will set the stage for a flood of industry concessions [such as financial payments to the states and restrictions on cigarette advertising and promotions]," stated Massachusetts attorney general Scott Harshbarger.

Even though Liggett & Myers had made numerous concessions, its directors hailed the settlement as a victory for the company, and for the industry as a whole. They claimed it finally removed the longer-term risk of far greater financial damages and concessions.

"The tobacco industry," asserted L&M chairman and CEO Bennett LeBow, "has lived for too long with the possibility of financial [ruin] from product liability suits that could destroy the industry. The settlement is a fresh and prudent approach to this problem and positively addresses concerns about underage smoking."

To some extent LeBow is correct in his assessment, because the terms of the settlement mean that smokers covered by the Castano class action—that is, virtually all American smokers—cannot sue Liggett & Myers in the future. However, this settlement does not protect L&M from lawsuits addressing the effects of secondhand smoke.

In May 1996 a federal appeals court dismissed *Castano v. American Tobacco*. The three-judge panel ruled that because laws regarding class action suits varied from state to state the Castano case was too complex to be argued in federal court. The tobacco industry was overjoyed, but attorneys for the plaintiffs were not discouraged. They promptly pledged to start class action lawsuits in each of the fifty state court systems. That could mean increased trouble for the industry. "Instead of fighting this case in one court," says David Vladeck of the Public Citizen Litigation Group, an antismoking group, "they will be fighting them in fifty."

A question of rights and responsibilities

The legal battles over smoking reveal how complex the issue of smoking has become. Many competing rights and responsibilities are involved. For example, smokers have the right to use a legal product such as cigarettes, but nonsmokers have the right not to inhale other people's sec-

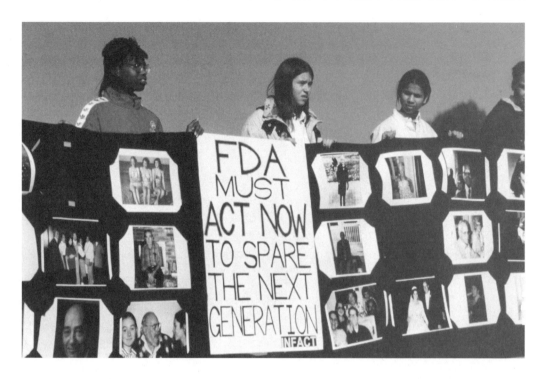

ondhand smoke. Tobacco companies have the right to advertise a legal product, but that right can be restricted for the public good. Society has a responsibility to protect its members from dangerous, even deadly, products and from substances that may prove to be addictive. Cigarette manufacturers contend that as no one has proved their product is dangerous, deadly, or addictive, they have the right to continue marketing it.

The stakes are very high. Tobacco companies take in billions of dollars in revenues each year from cigarette sales, and they directly and indirectly employ hundreds of thousands of American workers. At the same time, more than three hundred thousand people die each year from smoking-related diseases. The government spends millions of dollars to condemn smoking, yet at the same time it collects billions of dollars in taxes from the sale of tobacco products. As a result of these warring interests, smoking promises to remain the focus of many political and health debates in America for years to come.

This demonstration urges the FDA to restrict cigarette marketing to youth. In March 1996 Liggett & Myers agreed to some of the FDA's proposals to prevent teen smoking.

Organizations to Contact

Action on Smoking and Health
2013 H St. NW
Washington, DC 20006
(202) 659-4310
Web site: http://www.setinc.com/ash

Action on Smoking and Health is a pioneer antismoking organization founded in 1967 by its executive director, John F. Banzhof III. Originally formed to defend television's Fairness Doctrine, which provided for televised antismoking messages, it has since moved on to examining the full range of tobacco-related questions.

American Cancer Society
Tower Place
3340 Peachtree Rd. NE
Atlanta, GA 30026
(404) 320-3333
(800) ACS-2345
Web site: http://www.cancer.org

Because of the links between tobacco and cancer, the American Cancer Society has been a leader in antismoking initiatives, but it also deals with all forms of cancer, no matter what the cause. Founded in 1913 by ten doctors and five laymen, the organization now has two million members, fifty-seven divisions, and thirty-four hundred local branches.

American Heart Association (AHA)
7272 Greenville Ave.
Dallas, TX 75231-4596
(800) 242-8721
Web site: http://www.amhrt.org

The American Heart Association's main goal is to reduce the incidence of cardiovascular diseases such as heart attack and stroke. Its public awareness program warns of the dangers of tobacco and it sponsors research on the effects of tobacco use. The AHA has twenty-two hundred state and local metropolitan affiliates and is assisted by 3.7 million volunteers.

American Lung Association (ALA)
1740 Broadway
New York, NY 10019-4374
(212) 315-8700
(800) LUNG-USA
fax: (212) 265-5642

Founded in 1904 to combat tuberculosis, the American Lung Association has long studied lung diseases. Like other health organizations it warns against smoking. Along with its medical section, the American Thoracic Association, the ALA fights all forms of lung disease through research and professional education, prevention and school programs, environmental health programs, and advocacy programs.

Americans for Non-Smokers' Rights
2530 San Pablo Ave., Avenue J
Berkeley, CA 94702
(510) 841-3032
fax: (510) 841-3071
e-mail: anr@no-smoke.org
Web site: http://www.no-smoke.org

Americans for Non-Smokers' Rights is the only national nonprofit lobbying organization fighting to protect nonsmokers from secondhand smoke and to protect minors from becoming addicted to tobacco. It also maintains the American Non-smokers' Rights Foundation, which creates programs for schoolchildren on the issues of smoking prevention and secondhand smoke. The foundation also works with adults in promoting smoke-free environments.

Coalition on Smoking OR Health
1150 Connecticut Ave. NW, Suite 820
Washington, DC 20036
(202) 452-1184
fax: (202) 452-1417

The Coalition on Smoking OR Health, a cooperative venture of the American Cancer Society, the American Lung Association, and the American Heart Association, has published studies on such topics as teen smoking, clean indoor air, increasing taxes on tobacco products, and state tobacco legislation.

Friends of Tobacco
403-B East New Bern Rd.
Kinston, NC 28501
(919) 522-GROW
Web site: http://www.fujipub.com.fot

Friends of Tobacco supports tobacco growers' concerns and also deals with a number of other tobacco-related issues from a pro-smoking standpoint. Friends of Tobacco states it "will work with all friends of tobacco to preserve tobacco economics for our nation and freedom of choice."

National Smokers Alliance (NSA)
901 N. Washington St., Suite 400
Alexandria, VA 22314
(703) 739-1324

NSA, a nonprofit membership organization, is a lesser-known but very active pro-tobacco group, arguing for smokers' rights. It claims 3 million members. It opposes government bans on smoking in public areas and what it terms discrimination against smokers and excessive taxation of tobacco products.

The Tobacco Institute
1875 I St. NW
Washington, DC 20006
(202) 822-3393

The Tobacco Institute, closely allied with the tobacco industry, is the most powerful and effective pro-smoking organization. Founded in the 1950s, it is the oldest and perhaps best-known and best-funded pro-tobacco group.

Suggestions for Further Reading

Margaret O. Hyde, *Know About Smoking*. New York: Walker and Co., 1990.

Robert Perry, *Focus on Nicotine and Caffeine*. Illustrated by David Neuhaus. Frederick, MD: Twenty-First Century Books, 1990.

U.S. Department of Health and Human Services, *SGR4Kids: The Surgeon General's Report for Kids About Smoking*. Washington, DC: U.S. Government Printing Office, 1994.

Brian R. Ward, *Smoking and Health*. New York: Franklin Watts, 1986.

Works Consulted

Carl E. Bartecchi, Thomas D. MacKenzie, and Robert W. Schrier, "The Global Smoking Epidemic," *Scientific American*, May 1995.

William Booth, "Florida Sues Tobacco Firms to Recover Health Costs," *Washington Post*, February 22, 1995.

Anne Borgman, "Trying to Snuff Out Teens' Tobacco Use," *Washington Post*, July 6, 1995.

B. Bruce-Biggs, "The Health Police Are Blowing Smoke," *Fortune*, April 25, 1988.

Dan Colburn, "Chewing Tobacco," *Washington Post*, October 19, 1993.

Lewis Cope, "Tobacco Timeline and Minnesota's Role," *Minneapolis Star Tribune*, July 17, 1994.

Thomas DiBacco, "Smoke Puffery, Then and Now," *Associated Press Report*, August 23, 1994.

Margaret Ebrahim and Charles Lewis, "Will Washington Kick Tobacco?" *Nation*, April 25, 1994.

William Eckenbarger, "The Strange History of Tobacco," *Reader's Digest*, April 1992.

Paul Farhi, "Deadly Toll Closing the Gender Gap," *Washington Post*, May 23, 1992.

Christopher John Farley, "The Butt Stops Here," *Time*, April 18, 1994.

Michael Fumento, "Is EPA Blowing Its Own Smoke: How Much Science Is Behind Its Tobacco Finding?" *Investors Business Daily*, January 23, 1993.

Lila Gano, *Smoking*. San Diego: Lucent Books, 1989.

Malcolm Gladwell, "Court Reverses Ruling in Smoking Death," *Washington Post*, January 6, 1990.

David Hosansky, "Weeded Out," *New Republic*, April 22, 1996.

Gary L. Huber, Robert E. Brockie, and Vijay K. Mahajan, "Passive Smoking: How Great a Hazard?" *Consumers' Research*, July 1991.

———, "Smoke and Mirrors: The EPA's Flawed Study of Environmental Tobacco Smoke and Lung Cancer," *Regulation*, no. 3, 1993.

Vicki Kemper, "The Inhalers," *Common Cause Magazine*, Spring 1995.

Tom Kenworthy and David Brown, "Tobacco Firms Sue EPA on Cancer Ruling," *Washington Post*, June 23, 1993.

Richard Klein, *Cigarettes Are Sublime*. Durham, NC: Duke University Press, 1993.

Horace R. Kornegay, "The Cigarette Controversy," *Engage/Social Action*, September 1980.

David Landis, "Smoking and Bone Loss," *USA Today*, April 17, 1991.

Richard Leonard, *Should Tobacco Advertising and Promotion Be Banned?* New York: American Lung Association, 1991.

Tony Mauro, "'New Day' But No Guarantee in Cigarette Suits," *USA Today*, June 25, 1992.

———, "Tobacco Industry Faces Test of Liability in Deaths," *USA Today*, October 8, 1991.

Minneapolis Star Tribune, "Judge Clears Way for Millions to Sue Tobacco Firms," February 2, 1985.

———, "Philip Morris Rebuts Charges," March 21, 1996.

Morton Mintz, "Jury Finds Tobacco Firm Shares Blame in Death," *Washington Post*, June 14, 1988.

———, "Marketing Tobacco to Children," *Nation*, May 6, 1991.

Joyce Murdoch, "Where There's Smoke . . . Tobacco Becomes Taboo," *Washington Post*, February 21, 1993.

Dan Oldenburg, "Tobacco's Last Gasp?" *Washington Post*, February 23, 1993.

Kim Painter, "Smoking Can Cause Risk of Osteoporosis," *USA Today*, March 5, 1991.

Janet Raloff, "Cigarettes: Are They Doubly Addictive?" *Science News*, May 7, 1994.

Reuter Press Report, "Court Begins Hearing Tobacco-Medicaid Lawsuit," December 19, 1994.

———, "Judge Changes Scope of Florida Lawsuit," June 19, 1995.

———, "Lawmakers Move to Limit Tobacco's Nicotine," June 16, 1995.

Carl Ryan, "Do Films Push Cigarettes?" *Washington Times*, December 18, 1994.

Dodi Schultz, *Lung Disease Data 1995*. New York: American Lung Association, 1995.

John Schwartz, "Despite ABC Apology, FDA to Keep Up Campaign," *Washington Post*, August 27, 1995.

———, "FDA Chief Discloses High-Nicotine Leaf," *Washington Post*, June 22, 1994.

———, "Teenagers Smoking More, Survey Shows," *Washington Post*, July 20, 1995.

Charles Scriven, "A Tax We Can Live With," *Christianity Today*, March 8, 1993.

Jay Siwik, "Dangers of Secondhand Smoke," *Washington Post*, December 14, 1993.

Gordon Slovut, "State, Blue Cross Sue Tobacco Industry," *Minneapolis Star Tribune*, August 18, 1994.

Jill Smolowe, "Need a Place to Puff?" *Time*, April 18, 1994.

Paul Span, "The War over a Smoker's Death," *Washington Post*, May 27, 1988.

Sally Squires, "Smoking: The Evidence Mounts," *Washington Post*, June 28, 1988.

Gary Strauss, "Price Cut Designed to Bring Back Smokers," *USA Today*, April 5, 1993.

Time, "Camels for Kids," December 23, 1991.

———, "Litigation: Stubbed, But Not Out," January 15, 1990.

———, "Litigation: Where There's Smoke . . .," April 8, 1991.

———, "A Patch of Hope for Smokers," December 23, 1991.

———, "A Surprising Display of Centrist Thinking," July 16, 1992.

Saundra Torry and John Schwartz, "Tobacco Firms Win in Court," *Washington Post*, May 24, 1996.

Anastasia Toufexis, "Are Smokers Junkies?" *Time*, March 21, 1994.

———, "Is It All Over for Smokers?" *Time*, April 18, 1994.

U.S. Department of Health and Human Services, *The Health Consequences of Involuntary Smoking*. Washington, DC: U.S. Government Printing Office, 1986.

———, *The Health Consequences of Smoking: Nicotine Addiction*. Washington, DC: U.S. Government Printing Office, 1988.

———, *Preventing Tobacco Use Among Young People: A Report of the Surgeon General*. Washington, DC: U.S. Government Printing Office, 1994.

———, *Reducing the Health Consequences of Smoking: 25 Years of Progress*. Washington, DC: U.S. Government Printing Office, 1989.

U.S. News & World Report, "Why Teens Refuse to Give Up Smoking: Peer Pressure Often Overwhelms Good Sense," August 7, 1995.

Arlene Vigoda, "Smoking Report," *USA Today*, May 11, 1990.

Kenneth E. Warner and George A. Fulton, "The Economic Implications of Tobacco Product Sales in a Nontobacco State," *JAMA*, March 9, 1994.

Washington Post, "Anti-Smoking Ads Warn Women of Exploitation," September 8, 1992.

———, "Anti-Tobacco Lawsuits Move to State Courts," May 25, 1996.

———, "Two Wins for Tobacco," May 25, 1996.

Garry Wills, "Bob Dole and Tobacco's Big Lies," *New York Post*, June 25, 1996.

Robert Woessner, "Smoking Ads Called Misleading," *USA Today*, May 1, 1992.

Index

acetaldehyde
  addictive properties of, 36
Action on Smoking and Health,
  53, 54
addiction
  acetaldehyde and, 36
  nicotine and, 35
advanced glucation
  endproducts (AGE), 26
advertising, 70
  first use of, 12, 15
  free speech and, 73–75
Agricultural Adjustment Act,
  16
airlines
  smoking restrictions by,
  53–54
American Civil Liberties
  Union, 73
  tobacco industry and, 74
American Journal of Cancer,
  21
American Lung Association, 6,
  35
American Tobacco Company,
  83, 91
animal experiments, 30–31

Bacon, Diane, 59
Banzhof, John, 61
bronchitis, 22–23
Brown & Williamson, 35, 39
Browner, Carol, 49

Bruce-Biggs, B., 31
Burney, Leroy E., 22
Byrd, William, 11

Carnes, Betty, 54
Carter, Jimmy, 81
Carter, Peggy, 41, 73
*Castano v. American Tobacco
  Co.*, 91, 94
cataracts, 28
Chicago Anti-Cigarette League,
  13, 15
children
  risks of secondhand smoke to,
  50–52
cigarettes
  advertising of, 12, 15, 70
  brand-switching argument
    for, 70–72
  distribution during World
    War I, 12–13, 43
  invention of, 11
  nicotine content in, 34
  as nicotine delivery vehicle,
    40–41
  vending machine sales of,
    77–78
  warning labels on, 28–29, 44
Cipollone, Rose, 84–86
Ciraulo, Dominec, 36
Civilian Aviation Board, 53
Clinton, Bill, 19, 81
  on Joe Camel campaign, 73

Coalition on Smoking and
  Health, 39, 76
Common Cause, 18
Competitive Enterprise
  Institute, 63
confidence interval, 63
Congressional Research
  Service, 61
Copenhagen Male Study, 31

Dawson, Brennan, 40
Department of Health,
  Education, and Welfare
  (HEW), 54
Dole, Bob, 36
Durbin, Dick, 18

Ecenbarger, William, 32
Edell, Marc, 87
Elders, Joycelyn, 50
emphysema, 23
Environmental Protection
  Agency, 6, 47
  classification of secondhand
    smoke by, 49
  on secondhand smoke
    dangers, 47–49
    to children, 51
    criticism of study by, 61–63
environmental tobacco smoke
  composition of, 47–48
  dangers of
    to children, 50–52
    doubts about, 61–63
    smokers' rights and, 64,
      94–95
  efforts to control, 52–53
  EPA classification of, 49
  financial costs of, 49
  sudden infant death syndrome
    and, 52

Federal Trade Commission, 76
First Amendment, 75
Food and Drug Administration
  (FDA), 35, 39
  classification of nicotine as
    drug by, 45–46
  proposals to limit teen
    smoking, 78–81
Foote, Emerson, 71
Fortune magazine, 31

Gaston, Lucy Page, 13, 15, 21
Glantz, Seymore, 63
Glantz, Stanton A., 68
Graham, Evarts A., 21–22
Gravelle, Jane G., 61
Greenfield, Jeff, 68
*Green v. American Tobacco
  Co.*, 82–83

Harshbarger, Scott, 94
heart disease, 7, 25–26
  secondhand smoke and, 49–50
Heritage Foundation, 63
Hoffman, Matthew C., 63
Holmes, Oliver Wendell, Jr., 75
Hughes, Lloyd "Spud," 15
Humphrey, Hubert, III, 89

Interstate Commerce
  Commission, 54

Jerez, Rodrigo de, 10, 42
Joe Camel campaign, 72
  banning of, 76
    would violate First
      Amendment, 74–75
*Journal of Bone and Mineral
  Research*, 28
*Journal of the American
  College of Cardiology*, 49

Journal of the American Medical Association (JAMA), 22, 27, 52

Kennedy, John F., 22
Kessler, David, 39, 46
Koop, C. Everett, 18
Kornegay, Horace R., 31

LeBow, Bennett, 94
Liggett & Meyers, 82, 92
  concessions by, 93–94
Lippman, Morton, 64
Loman, Marianne, 59
Lorillard Tobacco, 91
lung cancer
  first rise in incidence of, 21
  secondhand smoke and, 48–49

Meyerson, David, 26
Minnesota Blue Cross, 89
Minnesota Clean Indoor Air Act, 54
Moore, Mike, 89

National Anti-Cigarette League, 13
National Cancer Institute, 63
Native Americans, 10
Neilson, David R., 51
New York Times Magazine, 19
nicotine
  addictive nature of, 35
  classification as drug, 44–46
  levels in cigarettes, 34, 37
    manipulation of, 38–40
Noble, Victor, 41

Ochsner, Alton, 20
Office on Smoking and Health (OSH), 18

Philip Morris Companies, 41, 46, 91
Pickower Institute, 26
political action committees (PACs), 18
preemption, 86
pregnancy
  smoking during, 23–25
Pritchett v. Liggett & Meyers, 82
Public Citizen Litigation Group, 94
Pure Food and Drug Act, 82–83

Reader's Digest, 32
Reilly, William K., 49
Respiratory Health Effects of Passive Smoking: Lung Cancer and Other Diseases (EPA), 47
Richardson, Elliot, 54
R. J. Reynolds, 40, 41, 91
  Joe Camel advertising campaign, 72–73
Roosevelt, Franklin D., 15, 21
Rose, Charlie, 63
Rosenblatt, Roger, 19

Sandefur, Thomas, 35–36
Schoendorf, Kenneth C., 52
secondhand smoke. *See* environmental tobacco smoke
Shalala, Donna, 65
Shanahan, John, 63
smokers
  fatalism of, 31
  rights of, 58–59
    secondhand smoke issue and, 64, 94–95

tobacco industry support of,
  60–61
smoking
  addictive nature of, 32–33
  celebrity endorsement of,
    15–16, 68–69
  costs of, 7
  early history of, 10–12
  pregnancy and, 23–25
  restrictions on
    by private businesses, 56–58
    by states and municipalities,
      54–56
    by teenagers
      increase in, 65–66
      reasons for, 66–67
sudden infant death syndrome
  (SIDS)
  link with parental smoking, 52
*Surgeon General's Report on
  Smoking and Tobacco* (1964),
  28, 44

Teague, Claude, 41
teenagers
  smoking among
    increase in, 65–66
    reasons for, 66–67
  targeting of, by tobacco
    companies, 67, 76–77
Terry, Luther, 22, 28
Thompson, Carol, 8
tobacco
  growing
    in American colonies, 10–11
    government support of,
      16–18

regulation of, 42–43
  by FDA, 45–46
taxation of, 43–44
types of, 37
tobacco companies
  absolute liability of, 84
  lawsuits against, 82–87
    by states, 87–89
  nicotine level manipulation
    by, 38–40
  political influence of, 18–19
  preemption defense of, 86–87
Tobacco Institute, 39, 92
Torres, Luis de, 10
Tribe, Lawrence, 87
Tufts University, 28, 36

University of Michigan Study,
  64–66
USA Today, 6, 81
U.S. Department of Agriculture
  (USDA), 16

Vigoda, Arlene, 6
Vladeck, David, 94

Ward, Scott, 66
Washington, George, 11
Washington Post, 59
Waxman, Henry, 18, 49, 61
Wilks v. American Tobacco Co.,
  84
women
  increase in smoking by, 14–15
  lung cancer increase among,
    21
Wynder, Ernst, 22

About the Author

David Pietrusza has written for numerous publications, including *Modern Age*, the *Journal of Social and Political Studies*, *Academic Reviewer*, and the *New Oxford Review*. He is the author of *The End of the Cold War*, *The Invasion of Normandy*, *The Battle of Waterloo*, *John F. Kennedy*, and *The Chinese Cultural Revolution*, previously published by Lucent.

Mr. Pietrusza has also written extensively on the subject of sports. He is the president of the Society for American Baseball Research (SABR), managing editor of *Total Baseball*, the official encyclopedia of Major League Baseball, and coeditor of the books *Total Braves* and *Total Indians*. He has written five books on baseball (*Judge and Jury: The Life and Times of Judge Kenesaw Mountain Landis, Lights On!, Minor Miracles, Major Leagues*, and *Baseball's Canadian-American League*) and one on basketball (*The Phoenix Suns*). In 1994 Mr. Pietrusza served as a consultant for the PBS Learning Link on-line system and produced the documentary *Local Heroes* for PBS affiliate WMHT.

He lives with his wife, Patricia, in Scotia, New York.

Picture Credits